At Issue

Wrongful Conviction
and Exoneration

Other Books in the At Issue Series

At Issue

Wrongful Conviction and Exoneration

Lisa Idzikowski, Book Editor

GREENHAVEN PUBLISHING

Published in 2020 by Greenhaven Publishing, LLC
353 3rd Avenue, Suite 255, New York, NY 10010

Copyright © 2020 by Greenhaven Publishing, LLC

First Edition

Articles in Greenhaven Publishing anthologies are often edited for length to meet page
requirements. In addition, original titles of these works are changed to clearly present
the main thesis and to explicitly indicate the author's opinion. Every effort is made to
ensure that Greenhaven Publishing accurately reflects the original intent of the authors.
Every effort has been made to trace the owners of the copyrighted material.

Cover image: Steve Maztker/Chicago Tribune/TNS via Getty Images

Library of Congress Cataloging-in-Publication Data

Names: Idzikowski, Lisa, editor.
Title: Wrongful conviction and exoneration / Lisa Idzikowski, book editor.
Description: New York : Greenhaven Publishing, 2020. | Series: At issue |
 Includes bibliographical references and index. | Audience: Grades 9–12.
Identifiers: LCCN 2019001966| ISBN 9781534505155 (library bound) | ISBN
 9781534505162 (pbk.)
Subjects: LCSH: Judicial error—United States—Juvenile literature.
Classification: LCC KF9756 .W758 2019 | DDC 345.73/0122—dc23
LC record available at https://lccn.loc.gov/2019001966

Manufactured in the United States of America

Website: http://greenhavenpublishing.com

Contents

Introduction

B anks are robbed. People are mugged. Thieves grab electronics or jewelry. Drunk drivers slam into other vehicles. Innocent people are caught in the crossfire of drive-by shootings. Deranged terrorists plow through crowds. Crime seems to be everywhere we turn, especially when considering the way it is reported almost nonstop by news stations, social media, and TV broadcasts. Crime victims and people in general typically expect that perpetrators will be prosecuted and punished, but how frequently does this happen? What's more, are all individuals tried and deemed guilty by the justice system truly guilty of the crimes for which they are convicted? And if not, are these individuals ever exonerated—released from prison and absolved of responsibility for the crime that led to their conviction? What happens to them if they are?

Two important questions come to mind when considering conviction: Do innocent people get convicted, and how often do innocent people get wrongfully convicted? Experts say that no justice system is infallible, and that mistakes are made. In a piece for the *Chicago Tribune*, John Grisham stated that somewhere between two and ten percent of convicted individuals were wrongfully convicted.[1] That may sound like a low percentage, but this translates to a large number of people in the United States: between 46,000 and 230,000. Grisham adds, "Once an innocent person is convicted, it is next to impossible to get the individual out of prison."

Some countries have better track records when it comes to maintaining a fair and appropriate system of justice. Country-specific laws and international laws attempt to protect the innocent. But even with these safeguards, wrongful convictions occur for a variety of reasons. What could possibly account for an innocent person being mistakenly tried in court and determined guilty? According to the Innocence Project, several things may bring this about. Estimates on exonerated individuals show that roughly one in four gave false confessions, admitting they committed the crime despite being innocent. People who give false confessions are often confused, afraid, frustrated, and sometimes exhausted from being interrogated—they want the questioning to stop. Interestingly, false confessions occur in particularly high rates in cases of murder.

Poorly completed forensics can also affect convictions, and according to the Innocence Project it is the second most common reason for wrongful convictions, as it is a factor in about 44 percent of them.[2] Some forensic evidence is unreliable, such as bite mark identification. Others—such as shoeprint evidence—have not been studied enough to be considered valid. Poor forensic evidence can also be traced to human error or deliberate intentions to mislead or commit fraud in testimony. Changes in scientific principles, especially surrounding DNA evidence, have rapidly occurred, but not all community jurisdictions have kept up to date and may unintentionally use unreliable forensic techniques. Other reasons, such as police misconduct, jailhouse informants, and incompetent misrepresentation or bad lawyering, account for other wrongful convictions.

Studies show that the biggest factor leading to wrongful conviction is witness misidentification. Experts at the Innocence Project state that witness misidentification is a major contributing factor to unjust conviction. In the more than 350 wrongful conviction cases overturned by DNA evidence, approximately 70 percent of those wrongful convictions occurred because of witness misidentification.[2]

Clearly, in the United States—the country with the highest incarceration rate in the world as shown by the Prison Policy Initiative—many individuals suffer because they have been wrongfully convicted and are serving prison terms unjustly.[3] Are they the only persons who suffer because of this social injustice? Documented cases show that crime victims often suffer in two different ways. At the time of the crime, victims suffer in the ways one would suspect. But interestingly, if their attackers are later judged to be innocent, they often suffer again. When the now-innocent individuals are released from imprisonment, the victim often feels regret, guilt, and fear because they were involved in an an innocent person being sentenced in the first place. Often, fear is also a result because, they reason, the newly freed individual will want to seek revenge, come after them, and inflict bodily harm.

Ultimately, what becomes of the individuals that are exonerated? There appears to be a wide range of experiences for those who are deemed innocent and released from prison. States vary in terms of the laws that govern treatment of exonerated persons. Some provide appropriate support so that an individual can return to as normal of an existence as possible. But in other states the support may be little, if there is any at all. When initially taken into custody and tried, one has to pay legal fines and fees. The justice system is costly, and someone has to pay. But what happens if a guilty verdict is overturned? Does that mean the judged innocent will recoup their expenses? Not always. Sometimes the wrongly accused receives nothing in return, and sometimes they do get reimbursed, but only after a long and agonizing process.

Consider what happens after someone is imprisoned for any number of years and then is exonerated of his or her crime. How does he or she get by after being released? Once again, the situation varies greatly from case to case, and the experience differs between individuals. Some people have reported that they are given a compensation package including money for the time lost in prison. Others have received little or no "back pay." According to the Innocence Project, on average it takes an exoneree about three years to receive any compensation after they are released.[4] If they do receive a monetary benefit, roughly 81 percent have reported that it is less than $50,000 for each year they were wrongfully imprisoned, and about 25 percent have reported getting nothing at all. Not surprisingly, most of the exonerees say that they would give anything to get back the time they lost in prison.

Clearly the topic of wrongful conviction and the compensation owed to exonerated individuals is a source of controversy. As with any controversial topic, committed proponents, opponents, activists, and experts have various perspectives on the topic. The viewpoints in *At Issue: Wrongful Conviction and Exoneration* debate and shed light on this important issue.

Notes

1. John Grisham, "Commentary: Why the Innocent End Up in Prison," *Chicago Tribune*, March 14, 2018, https://www.chicagotribune.com/news/opinion/commentary/ct -perspec-innocent-prisoners-innocence-project-death-row-dna-testing-prosecutors -0315-story.html.

2. "DNA Exoneration in the United States," Innocence Project, https://www .innocenceproject.org/dna-exonerations-in-the-united-states/.

3. Peter Wagner and Wendy Sawyer, "States of Incarceration: The Global Context 2018," Prison Policy Initiative, June 2018, https://www.prisonpolicy.org/global/2018.html.

4. "81% of Exonerated People Who Have Been Compensated Under State Laws Received Less Than the Federal Standard, New Innocence Project Report Shows," Innocence Project, December 2, 2009, https://www.innocenceproject.org/81-of-exonerated -people-who-have-been-compensated-under-state-laws-received-less-than-the-federal -standard-new-innocence-project-report-shows/.

1

Wrongful Convictions Are Caused by Various Factors

Centurion.org

Centurion.org is an organization that is dedicated to freeing wrongly convicted men and women serving life or death sentences.

There are various reasons why people are wrongly convicted of crimes. Misidentification by the witness is one reason. There are also a number of factors that could cause witnesses to misidentify a person: memory is not perfect, and perceptions fail under various environmental variables. False confession is another major factor that deserves examination, as innocent people frequently confess to committing crimes. Botched forensic evidence and police misconduct are other notable contributors to improper convictions of innocent people. The final two reasons examined by this viewpoint are jailhouse informers and inept lawyers.

Eyewitness Misidentification

Eyewitness identification is often the most powerful 'evidence' in a case as victims of crimes can unknowingly exaggerate the time they had to see an assailant and exaggerate lighting conditions. There is an ingrained belief that our brain works like a tape recorder and if we think hard enough we can remember what we saw. The truth is; memory is a confabulation of smells, sounds, other memories, along with what you think you saw. As Elizabeth Loftus a pioneer in the witness identification work once said, "we should not be

"Causes of Wrongful Convictions," Centurion.org. Reprinted by permission.

surprised when a witness gets an identification wrong, we should be surprised when they get it right."

Often crimes happen at night and in poorly lit areas, and our vision actually diminishes when we are frightened. So a victim of a violent crime is often at a terrible disadvantage for seeing and remembering the assailant. Not to mention crimes usually happen quickly and in a fluid manner, again, not ideal for seeing and remembering. And cross racial identification has been proven to be vulnerable to a high rate of error. We have also learned that line ups and mug shot spreads are really just a platform for guessing. Sequential identification has proven to be far less error prone, but much of law enforcement is not happy with it because it does not lead to a lot of arrests.

We need to be highly critical in our thinking when we hear of an eyewitness to a crime identifying someone.

False Confession

Among the many themes in wrongful convictions, one of the most difficult for the public, prosecutors, defense lawyers, judges and juries to understand are false confessions. The prevailing wisdom is that innocent people do not confess to crimes they did not commit. It is a statistical fact that the opposite is true, 25% of those exonerated through DNA testing had falsely confessed and statistics show that murder cases have a very high prevalence of false confessions.

People falsely confess for many reasons, primarily because they want the interrogation to stop. Contrary to public belief as proselytized by television programs: police interviews of suspects are not a search for truth or to gain insight; rather they are going to interrogate you in order to obtain a confession because they have a preconceived decision that you are the perpetrator. If you are in the clutches of the police to "talk" to them about a crime, they already have decided you are a suspect and are foreclosed to anything you have to say; other than that you did it.

False confessions are not the sole sector of the intellectually challenged. Anyone can falsely confess. Exhaustion, fear, frustration, confusion, and innocence are all the ingredients for a false confession. The police are very skilled in obtaining confessions and their belief in their own intuition blinds them to any information that does not fit their biased scenario about the suspect. What is astonishing is that there are not more false confessions.

And finally, the false confession is just the beginning. Saying 'I did it' is just the first step. The next step is the narrative. Police will work with the confessed to then create the story of how and why the crime was committed. They will feed the confessing suspect details that will form the story. This will be committed to paper and/or to video with a prosecutor which will be produced at the trial whether you testify or not. You can imagine how provocative that is to a jury and judge, and even a defense lawyer.

A very good scholarly readable book on the subject is Richard Leo's: *Police Interrogation and American Justice*.

Improper Forensics

There have been great advances made in exposing both deliberate and unintentional bad forensics. An example of unintentional bad forensics was the practice for years and years that "arson experts" were seasoned fire fighters who passed down folk wisdom in the guise of expertise concerning the characteristics of an arson fire and they were almost all wrong. The inadvertent list could include: fingerprint and ballistic testimony. The deliberate bad science list generally includes: bite mark testimony and shaken baby testimony.

Scientific expert's testimony naturally carries a lot of weight with a jury. For years and years their bad testimony carried the day and unfortunately it still does as too many defense lawyers have not done their homework and do not keep abreast of developments in criminology and forensics. Further, the burden is on the wrongly convicted whose cases rested on bad science to find organizations or experts and then lawyers, who can get their cases back into court. There is no immediate recourse for a case with outdated or bad forensics. Everything is a fight.

And then there are the cases that involve an unscrupulous forensic examiner. They are the toughest to deal with in that they have almost always been working hand and glove with prosecutors because the prosecutors know they can rely on them to give them results they need to get a conviction. It's almost unheard of to have a rogue scientist that is working without any support. Fortunately they are few and far between but the damage they cause is in the lives of the incarcerated, who often because of obfuscation by the courts and prosecutors, combined with an inability to find adequate representation, languish in prison for years before finding adequate assistance.

Police Misconduct

Without doing a statistical analysis we would guess that Prosecutorial Misconduct is an element in an extremely high percentage of wrongful convictions. In their zeal to obtain a conviction prosecutors turn a blind eye to problem witnesses and police reports or too often willfully join in the hiding of exculpatory evidence or allowing testimony to go forward they know is misleading at best and false at worst. Often the extent of the misconduct is not revealed until a civil suit is filed by the exonerated inmate.

Informants & Snitches

Jail house informants are the secret weapon of prosecutors and police when they have a weak case. If a case against a defendant does not have corroborating forensics or witness testimony; a jail house confession is almost as good as the defendant confessing to police. Having an inmate come in and testify that the defendant confessed to him or her and their testimony at the trial is being given without any promise of a reduced sentence is seen by jurors as heroic. They are testifying because their conscience prods them to do so. It is baffling that in this day and age, jurors are so naive, but they are.

Prosecutors have become much more wily with the timing of the compensation bestowed on the jail house informant. There will not be any paperwork about a promise, but a promise was made and shortly after testifying one of several things happens: their sentence is reduced; they are moved to a much better prison; the next time they are arrested that crime goes unpunished or is significantly reduced; the list of possibilities is endless.

Bad Lawyering

In the United States you get the justice you can afford and most people caught up in the criminal justice system cannot afford good vigorous representation. What they will get is someone who passed the bar and has a backlog of other cases and no budget to hire experts or an investigator, and no time to study the case against a defendant. A zealous attack on a case is simply not possible.

Certainly some lawyers are simply bad lawyers, but I think that the majority of them would do a much better job given less cases and money to hire experts and investigators. But the playing field is not even at all. The police investigation and any forensic testing has been done by the same agency that pays the prosecutor, they are colleagues. Defense lawyers are working against the house. And public defender who is over worked and underfunded and mostly has guilty clients, has naturally become inured to a claim of innocence. They have heard it before and perhaps more frustrating; they have no funds to marshal an aggressive defense anyway.

2

Criminal Justice Systems Around the World Make Mistakes

The Cornell Center on the Death Penalty Worldwide

The Cornell Center on the Death Penalty Worldwide (DPW) is a project created and operated by Cornell Law School. It uses research, data, advocacy, and publishing to aid and prevent wrongful convictions.

Criminal justice systems must work to convict guilty people of crimes that are committed, but no system is perfect, and because of various imperfections innocent people suffer. A significant number of cases involve the death penalty, and around the world mistakes occur and people are wrongfully executed as a result. In some countries there is no money, time, or expertise to prevent innocent people from being convicted, and after being convicted, there is little or no chance of the truly wrongful convictions being overturned.

No criminal justice system is perfect, and fallibility leads to miscarriages of justice. Even when all the standards for a fair trial are upheld, wrongful convictions can occur. Many countries that practice capital punishment, however, do not meet these standards. For instance, in Japan, the prosecution's failure to disclose exculpatory evidence has led to a number of wrongful convictions[1]. In India, prosecutorial misconduct has also led to several high profile cases of wrongful convictions[2]. In

"Innocence and Wrongful Convictions," The Cornell Center on the Death Penalty Worldwide, March 14, 2016. Reprinted by permission.

China and the United States, torture and police misconduct have contributed to the conviction of innocent persons[3]. Inadequate legal representation, shoddy police investigations, eyewitness misidentification, racial prejudice, and falsified evidence are additional factors that contribute to wrongful convictions around the world.

In the case of the death penalty, victims of wrongful convictions pay the ultimate price. Innocent people have been convicted and sentenced to death in every region of the world. In the United States alone, 143 people have been released from death row since 1973 on grounds of innocence[4]. In Japan, four death row inmates were exonerated between 1983 and 1989[5]. In March 2014, Japan released a man believed to be the longest-serving death row inmate in the world after courts concluded that the evidence used against him was likely fabricated[6]. The discovery of several wrongful convictions of individuals sentenced to death prompted public outrage and, subsequently, legislative reform in China[7]. One of those wrongfully convicted was executed, which has led to a public debate about the abolition of the death penalty[8]. In Zimbabwe, a man was acquitted after being convicted of rape five years earlier. The High Court reasoned that his trial was "riddled with several and serious contradictions."[9]

In some countries, such as Malawi, police are poorly trained, and defense attorneys lack resources to investigate their clients' cases. Many attorneys do not meet their clients until the day of trial. This lack of training and resources creates an enormous risk of wrongful convictions. Moreover, most prisoners in Malawi are unable to appeal their convictions since defense counsel are not automatically assigned to handle appeals. The lack of exonerations in many African countries should not be taken as evidence that all who are convicted are guilty; rather, there are simply no resources available for post-conviction investigations that are essential to uncover exculpatory evidence.

The availability of more reliable DNA testing has been a major factor in the uncovering of false convictions in the United States, and DNA exonerations have revealed the startling inadequacies of criminal justice systems. DNA technology, however, is not a universally effective method to redress wrongful convictions. Genetic analysis requires resources and expertise which not always available in underfunded judicial systems. Moreover, many retentionist countries do not preserve biological samples under conditions that allow for post-conviction testing, and in some cases do not gather any at all.

In addressing wrongful convictions, national and international legal systems deal with front-end and back-end issues: (1) minimizing the potential for wrongful convictions in the first place and (2) compensating victims of wrongful convictions.

Prevention of Wrongful Convictions

The right to a fair trial is guaranteed under international law in order to protect individuals from unlawful detention and to minimize the possibility of wrongful convictions. Indeed, the UN Safeguards Protecting the Rights of Those Facing the Death Penalty states that capital punishment may only be carried out pursuant to a final judgment rendered by a competent court after legal process which gives all possible safeguards to ensure a fair trial, at least equal to those contained in the International Covenant on Civil and Political Rights. U.N. ECOSOC, Safeguards Guaranteeing Protection of the Rights of Those Facing the Death Penalty, para. 5, E.S.C. Res. 1984/50, U.N. Doc. E/1984/92, 1984/. International standards relating to a fair trial are constantly evolving, but include: the right to a fair hearing; the presumption of innocence; freedom from compulsory self-incrimination; the right to know the accusation; adequate time and facilities to prepare a defense; the right to legal assistance; the right to examine witnesses; the right to an interpreter; and the right to appeal in criminal cases.

Numerous human rights treaties and covenants affirm the need for a fair trial. Article 10 of the Universal Declaration of Human Rights states "everyone is entitled in full equality to a fair and public hearing by an independent and impartial tribunal, in the determination of his rights and obligations and of any criminal charge against him." The right to a fair trial is further guaranteed under Article 14 of the International Covenant on Civil and Political Rights (ICCPR), Article 6 of the European Convention on Human Rights, Article 8 of the American Convention on Human Rights, and Article 7 of the African Commission on Human and Peoples' Rights. Several commissions and courts have elaborated upon that right. See, e.g., European Court of Human Rights, *Golder v. the United Kingdom*, 18 Eur. Ct. H.R. (ser. A, 1975), Feb. 21, 1975.

Compensating Victims of Wrongful Convictions

Several international instruments provide for the right to compensation in the case of wrongful convictions. The International Covenant on Civil and Political Rights, for example, requires that states compensate wrongfully convicted individuals under article 14(6). Article 3 of the European Convention on Human Rights and Article 10 of the American Convention on Human Rights similarly require compensation. Furthermore, the Principles and Guidelines on the Right to a Fair Trial and Legal Assistance in Africa, endorsed by the African Commission on Human and People's Rights, require that victims of wrongful convictions be compensated. African Comm. on Human and Peoples' Rights, Principles and Guidelines on the Right to a Fair Trial and Legal Assistance in Africa, DOC/OS(XXX)247, 2001.

Generally, the right to compensation requires that there be a reversal or pardon of a final conviction, based on new, or newly discovered, facts that demonstrate that the conviction was unjust. The duty to compensate may not arise if the person somehow contributed to the wrongful decision. The terms and procedures of the compensation are to be established by national laws.

Under the ICCPR, States Parties meet their obligations under article 14(6) in one or more of the following ways: incorporating the article directly into domestic legislation to create a statutory right to compensation; conferring discretion to an administrative or judicial body to determine whether awards of compensation should be paid; and utilizing the general power of domestic governments to make *ex gratia* payments. In addition, in states that have adopted the First Optional Protocol to the ICCPR, victims of wrongful convictions may submit individual complaints to the UN Human Rights Committee when their right to compensation under Article 14 of the ICCPR is not respected.

Many national laws provide citizens with the right to seek review of unjust convictions and compensation for the damages they suffered—although most of the countries that have passed such legislation no longer apply the death penalty. In some countries, these rights are expressly enshrined in the Constitution. See, e.g., Constitution of Portugal, art. 29(6); Constitution of Italy, art. 24; Constitution of Brazil, art. 5(LXXV). The Constitution of Spain, for example, guarantees compensation if damages arise from judicial errors. See, e.g., Constitution of Spain, sec. 121, 1978. In others, like the United Kingdom, the rights are enshrined in specific acts. See, e.g., UK's Criminal Justice Act, sec. 133. The terms and conditions of the revision and the compensation are often outlined in the Codes of Criminal Procedure or in specific statutes. A few countries have instituted specific commissions that have the power to investigate and refer claims of wrongful convictions to a court. Scotland, England, Wales, Northern Island, and Norway, for example, have established a Criminal Cases Review Commission. The Scottish Criminal Cases Review Commission has referred 122 cases from its inception in 1999[11]. The United States has failed to adopt federal legislation to provide compensation to the wrongfully convicted. Still, some states have adopted compensation laws, and exonerated people are sometimes able to receive compensation through state laws or civil lawsuits.

Cases

- *Shilayayev v. Russia*, 9647/02, ECtHR, Oct. 6, 2005, http://hudoc.echr.coe.int. The ECtHR found a violation of Article 6 §1 of the European Convention on Human Rights (right to a fair trial) and of Article 1 of Protocol No. 1 to the Convention (right to property) in that a State took more than two years to pay the compensation that had been awarded for the petitioner's wrongful conviction and imprisonment.

- *Poghosyan and Baghdasaryan v. Armenia*, 22999/06, ECtHR, June 12 2012. The ECtHR found, unanimously, a violation of Article 3 of Protocol No. 7 to the ECHR (compensation for wrongful conviction) in that the national law did not provide for non-pecuniary damages. The Court stated that compensation is due even where the domestic law or practice does not provide for such compensation; and that the purpose of Article 3 of Protocol No. 7 is not merely to recover any pecuniary loss caused by wrongful conviction but also to provide a person convicted as a result of a wrongful conviction with compensation for any non-pecuniary damage such as distress, anxiety, inconvenience and loss of enjoyment of life.

References

[1] Kazuko Ito, Wrongful Convictions and Recent Criminal Justice Reform in Japan, p. 1252, *University of Cincinnati Law Review*, Sep. 8, 2013.

[2] Prayaag Akbar, Presumed Guilty: After 14 wasted years in prison, life begins anew, http://www.sunday-guardian.com/g20columnists/presumed-guilty-after-14-wasted-years-in-prison-life-begins-anew, last accessed Mar. 3, 2014.

[3] Fox News, China tries to curb miscarriages of justice as anger over torture, other abuses, grows, http://www.foxnews.com/world/2013/11/27/china-tries-to-curb-miscarriages-justice-as-anger-over-torture-other-abuses/, Nov. 27, 2013. Ken Armstrong, Steve Mills, and Maurice Possley, Coercive and Illegal Tactics Torpedo Scores of Cook County Murder Cases, http://www.chicagotribune.com/news/watchdog/chi-011216confession,0,1748927.story, Dec. 16, 2001.

[4] Death Penalty Information Center, the Innocence List, http://www.deathpenaltyinfo.org/innocence-list-those-freed-death-row, last accessed Feb. 18, 2014.

[5] Kazuko Ito, Wrongful Convictions and Recent Criminal Justice Reform in Japan, p. 1254, *University of Cincinnati Law Review*, Sep. 8, 2013.

[6] Kiroko Tabuchi, Soul-Searching as Japan Ends a Man's Decades on Death Row, *New York Times*, http://www.nytimes.com/2014/03/28/world/asia/freed-after-decades-on-death-row-man-indicts-justice-in-japan.html, Mar. 27, 2014.

[7] Wrongful Convictions Blog, Miscarriages in China Prompt New Guidelines, http://wrongfulconvictionsblog.org/2013/08/15/miscarriages-of-justice-in-china-prompt-new-guidelines/, Aug. 15, 2013.

[8]Patrick Boehler, China's top judge calls for fewer executions, *South China Morning Post*, http://www.scmp.com/news/china-insider/article/1332237/chinas-top-judge-calls-fewer-executions, Oct. 15, 2013.

[9]The Herald, High Court Upholds HIV+ Man's Rape Appeal, http://www.herald.co.zw/high-court-upholds-hiv-mans-rape-appeal/, Mar. 25, 2014.

[11]Scottish Criminal Review Commission, Case Statistics, http://www.sccrc.org.uk/casestatistics.aspx, last accessed Feb. 28, 2014.

3

An In-Depth Analysis of Eyewitness Misidentification

The Innocence Project

The Innocence Project is an organization that aims to reform the criminal justice system and use DNA to exonerate the wrongly convicted.

In the United States, eyewitness misidentification is the biggest cause of wrongful convictions, and more than 70 percent of those are eventually overturned by DNA evidence. For various reasons, when confronted with a lineup, eyewitnesses often make mistakes in identification. Sometimes mistakes happen because of the conduct of law enforcement. According to the Innocence Project, a number of reforms can be put in place to prevent these high rates of misidentification by witnesses from continuing.

E yewitness misidentification is the greatest contributing factor to wrongful convictions proven by DNA testing, playing a role in more than 70% of convictions overturned through DNA testing nationwide.

Mistaken Identifications Are the Leading Factor in Wrongful Convictions

Mistaken eyewitness identifications contributed to approximately 70% of the more than 350 wrongful convictions in the United States overturned by post-conviction DNA evidence.

"Eyewitness Misidentification," The Innocence Project. Reprinted by permission.

- Inaccurate eyewitness identifications can confound investigations from the earliest stages. Critical time is lost while police are distracted from the real perpetrator, focusing instead on building the case against an innocent person.
- Despite solid and growing proof of the inaccuracy of traditional eyewitness ID procedures—and the availability of simple measures to reform them—traditional eyewitness identifications remain among the most commonly used and compelling evidence brought against criminal defendants.

Traditional Eyewitness Identification Practices—And Problems

- In a standard lineup, the lineup administrator typically knows who the suspect is. Research shows that administrators often provide unintentional cues to the eyewitness about which person to pick from the lineup.
- In a standard lineup, without instructions from the administrator, the eyewitness often assumes that the perpetrator of the crime is one of those presented in the lineup. This often leads to the selection of a person despite doubts.
- In a standard lineup, the lineup administrator may choose to compose a live or photo lineup where non-suspect "fillers" do not match the witness's description of the perpetrator. When fillers are selected that do not resemble the witness's description, this can cause the suspect to stand out to a witness because of the composition of the lineup. This unintentional suggestion can lead an eyewitness to identify a particular individual in a photo array or lineup.
- In a standard lineup, the lineup administrator may not elicit or document a statement from a witness articulating their level of confidence in an identification made during the identification process. A witness's confidence can be particularly susceptible to influence by information provided to the witness after the identification process. Research shows

that information provided to a witness after an identification suggesting that the witness selected the right person can dramatically, yet artificially, increase the witness's confidence in the identification. Therefore it is critically important to capture an eyewitness's level of confidence at the point in time that an identification is made.

How to Improve the Accuracy of Eyewitness Identifications

The Innocence Project endorses a range of procedural reforms to improve the accuracy of eyewitness identification. These reforms have been recognized by police, prosecutorial and judicial experience, as well as national justice organizations, including the National Institute of Justice, the International Association of Chiefs of Police, the NAACP, and the American Bar Association. The benefits of these reforms are corroborated by over 30 years of peer-reviewed comprehensive research.

In October of 2014, the National Academy of Sciences (NAS), the nation's premier scientific entity, issued a groundbreaking report settling many long-debated areas of police practice. The report identified a set of scientifically-supported reform procedures, which have been promoted by the Innocence Project since the inception of its work in this area of police practice.

The following reforms form the basis of the Innocence Project's eyewitness identification reform package:

1. **The "Double-blind" Procedure/Use of a Blind Administrator:** A "double-blind" lineup is one in which neither the administrator nor the eyewitness knows who the suspect is. This prevents the administrator of the lineup from providing inadvertent or intentional verbal or nonverbal cues to influence the eyewitness to pick the suspect.

2. **Instructions:** "Instructions" are a series of statements issued by the lineup administrator to the eyewitness that deter

the eyewitness from feeling compelled to make a selection. They also prevent the eyewitness from looking to the lineup administrator for feedback during the identification procedure. One of the recommended instructions includes the directive that the suspect may or may not be present in the lineup.

3. **Composing the Lineup:** Suspect photographs should be selected that do not bring unreasonable attention to him. Non-suspect photographs and/or live lineup members (fillers) should be selected based on their resemblance to the description provided by the eyewitness—as opposed to their resemblance to the police suspect. Note, however, that within this requirement, the suspect should not unduly stand out from among the other fillers. (More detailed recommendations can be provided upon request by the Innocence Project.)

4. **Confidence Statements:** Immediately following the lineup procedure, the eyewitness should provide a statement, in his own words, that articulates the level of confidence he or she has in the identification made.

5. **The Lineup Procedure Should Be Documented:** Ideally, the lineup procedure should be electronically recorded. If this is impracticable, an audio or written record should be made.

4

DNA Evidence Can Help Bring About Justice

Elizabeth Webster

Elizabeth Webster is a professor of criminal justice and criminology at Loyola University and a former communications professional at the Innocence Project.

In some cases, people who have been convicted of a crime and imprisoned are later found innocent. Sometimes it is a clear-cut instance of wrongful conviction. In other cases, things aren't so clear. DNA evidence can offer help to the justice system in clearing those wrongfully convicted. The Innocence Project aims to do this, but is not always successful in its attempts. Fortunately, in the case of Thomas Haynesworth discussed in this viewpoint their efforts were successful, as he was exonerated in December 2011. What is worse is that some states and jurisdictions still cling to outdated and ineffective methods that can hamper investigations.

After 27 years of wrongful imprisonment, Thomas Haynesworth was released in March on his 46th birthday at the request of Virginia Governor Robert McDonnell. The Virginia Attorney General and two of the Commonwealth's attorneys support his exoneration. So why is the Innocence Project still fighting to prove his innocence?

Haynesworth's troubles began in early 1984, when a serial rapist began terrorizing women in Richmond, Virginia. Police

"Why DNA Is Not Enough," by Elizabeth Webster, Forensic Genetics Policy Initiative. Reprinted by permission.

apprehended Haynesworth, an 18-year-old with no criminal record, after one of the victims spotted him on the street and identified him as her attacker. His photo was shown to victims of similar crimes. Ultimately, five victims identified him.

Haynesworth protested, saying that he was innocent, but the eyewitness evidence compelled the juries. Haynesworth was convicted of two rapes and one attempted robbery and abduction. "I thought they were going to see that they made a mistake and correct it," he says. "It's been 27 years, and I'm still waiting."

Haynesworth was sentenced to 74 years in prison, which might have been the end of the story, if not for a lab technician named Mary Jane Burton. While Virginia courts and police agencies routinely lost or destroyed evidence, Burton took the extraordinary effort of saving cotton swabs and other evidence samples in her notebooks. Had Burton followed lab policy and returned all of the samples to the investigating agencies, all evidence in these cases would have been gone forever. The blood type testing, or serology, that Burton performed was not nearly as probative as DNA testing would later become.

The Innocence Project and others pushed for a review of Burton's case files. In response, then Virginia Gov. Warner launched a massive DNA review of convictions. Burton died in 1999 and never learned of the tremendous impact of her work; so far six wrongfully convicted Virginians were proven innocent because of her practice of preserving evidence. The review also led to DNA tests in Haynesworth's case.

The DNA testing cleared Haynesworth in one of the rape convictions. Moreover, the Department of Forensic Science matched the sperm sample to the genetic profile of a convicted rapist named Leon Davis. DNA testing on a second rape that Haynesworth was charged with, but not convicted of, also cleared Haynesworth and pointed to Davis. Biological evidence from Haynesworth's other two convictions, however, does not exist. In one of the convictions, documents show that evidence was destroyed. There never was any biological evidence available in the other conviction.

Profile of a Perpetrator

Davis was suspected of committing at least a dozen rapes in Richmond and Henrico County in 1984, and he is currently serving multiple life sentences for those crimes. Davis and Haynesworth lived in the same neighborhood; they resembled each other and were sometimes mistaken for each other.

In Haynesworth's first letter to the Innocence Project in 2005, he writes: "There is an inmate named Leon Davis who is in prison for some of the same things I'm charged with, and he was living down the street from me in Richmond, Virginia....I will bet my life this is the man who committed these crimes....Just get my DNA tested, and you will see I'm innocent of these crimes."

All of the crimes were perpetrated within the same one-mile radius and all shared the same modus operandi. If DNA testing proved that Davis committed two of the crimes, it follows logically that he committed them all.

Haynesworth now waits for a hearing with the Virginia Court of Appeals. Until then he is on parole and is a registered sex offender. He leaves his mother's house only to report to his job as an office technician with the Office of the Virginia Attorney General, Ken Cuccinnelli. Without a writ of innocence or a pardon, Haynesworth cannot be cleared.

Accepting DNA's Limitations

In 1992, the newly founded Innocence Project began taking cases from prisoners with claims of innocence whose cases were suitable for post-conviction DNA testing. By 2000, 67 people had been exonerated, and the organization was swamped with letters from prisoners seeking assistance. This trend has not slowed in 19 years. Today the organization receives over 3,000 letters a year and nearly 300 people have been exonerated.

Yet the total number of wrongful convictions surely surpasses this. Many wrongfully convicted prisoners have no DNA evidence to test. Over 20% of the cases closed by the Innocence Project since 2004 were closed because evidence had been lost or destroyed. Despite diligent searching, there just isn't a Mary Jane Burton in every state. Evidence preservation laws have become more commonplace, but many jurisdictions, even major metropolitan areas, still have hopelessly outdated paper-based systems.

If DNA evidence had existed in all three of Haynesworth's convictions, it could easily have proven his innocence of those crimes. In a sexual assault case in which a single perpetrator attacks a stranger, and consent is not an issue, the results are easily interpreted. When a real perpetrator, like Leon Davis, can be identified through a DNA database hit, it not only exonerates the innocent but also solves the crime.

As it stands, investigators and attorneys had to look carefully at the pattern of crimes in Haynesworth's cases to see if they were likely committed by the same perpetrator. Such cases have resulted in exoneration before. But what about those cases that are not suitable for DNA testing at all? Very few cases involve physical evidence that could be subjected to DNA testing, even among violent crimes.

Unlike any other type of evidence, DNA testing can conclusively prove innocence (or guilt) to an unprecedented degree of scientific certainty. But a system that depends on DNA testing alone to protect the innocent is a failed system. DNA illuminates the flaws in the criminal justice system; it does not eliminate them.

Those flaws include eyewitness misidentification; improper use of the forensic sciences or reliance on outdated or invalidated forensic methods; false confessions, admissions, and even guilty pleas; jailhouse informant testimony, and more. Simple, cost-effective reforms—improving police lineup procedures, for example, or mandating that all interrogations be recorded—can reduce the rate of wrongful convictions, and by extension, assist in the apprehension of real perpetrators. Some states have been slow to adopt these reforms.

Before DNA exonerations became common, criminal justice professionals struggled to understand the implications of the technology. DNA testing trumps all other types of evidence— whether it's a witness who swears that he could never forget a face, a co-defendants' confession, or a hair analyst who claims to have a match. Admitting that the system has devastated an innocent person's life is never easy. The only way to truly reconcile the loss is to learn from the wrongful conviction and make sure it never happens again.

The Innocence Project continues to advocate for Haynesworth's exoneration on the remaining two cases. With the complete support of law enforcement in Virginia we hope that day comes soon. When it does, there will be those who say that the criminal justice system works. They will celebrate the power of DNA to find justice. But 27 years of wrongful imprisonment is not justice, and DNA cannot erase those years. While Haynesworth was behind bars, the true perpetrator continued to commit brutal crimes; additional women were harmed. DNA cannot erase what happened to those crime victims. But if the criminal justice system learns from these errors and continues to adopt reforms that will prevent future injustice, then DNA can be rightfully thanked for leading the way.

5

The Past, Present, and Future of DNA Fingerprinting

Lutz Roewer

Dr. Lutz Roewer is the head of the department for the Institute of Legal Medicine and Forensic Sciences at Charité Universitätsmedizin Berlin.

DNA fingerprinting—also known as forensic DNA analysis—was first used in the United Kingdom in 1984, but it has evolved significantly since then. Technological evolution and innovation has allowed DNA fingerprinting to become increasingly accurate, but this unfortunately also means that many errors occurred in earlier uses. Dr. Roewer explains the science behind DNA fingerprinting along with its risks and benefits, offering suggestions on how forensic DNA analysis could be further improved in the years to come.

DNA fingerprinting, one of the great discoveries of the late 20th century, has revolutionized forensic investigations. This review briefly recapitulates 30 years of progress in forensic DNA analysis which helps to convict criminals, exonerate the wrongly accused, and identify victims of crime, disasters, and war. Current standard methods based on short tandem repeats (STRs) as well as lineage markers (Y chromosome, mitochondrial DNA) are covered and applications are illustrated by casework examples. Benefits and

"DNA Fingerprinting in Forensics: Past, Present, Future," by Lutz Roewer, BioMed Central Ltd., November 18, 2013, https://investigativegenetics.biomedcentral.com/articles/10.1186/2041-2223-4-22. Licensed under CC BY 2.0.

risks of expanding forensic DNA databases are discussed and we ask what the future holds for forensic DNA fingerprinting.

The Past—A New Method that Changed the Forensic World

"I've found it! I've found it," he shouted, running towards us with a test-tube in his hand. "I have found a re-agent which is precipitated by hemoglobin, and by nothing else," says Sherlock Holmes to Watson in Arthur Conan Doyle's first novel *A Study in Scarlet* from1886 and later: "Now we have the Sherlock Holmes' test, and there will no longer be any difficulty [...]. Had this test been invented, there are hundreds of men now walking the earth who would long ago have paid the penalty of their crimes."

The Eureka shout shook England again and was heard around the world when roughly 100 years later Alec Jeffreys at the University of Leicester, in UK, found extraordinarily variable and heritable patterns from repetitive DNA analyzed with multi-locus probes. Not being Holmes he refrained to call the method after himself but "DNA fingerprinting." Under this name his invention opened up a new area of science. The technique proved applicable in many biological disciplines, namely in diversity and conservation studies among species, and in clinical and anthropological studies. But the true political and social dimension of genetic fingerprinting became apparent far beyond academic circles when the first applications in civil and criminal cases were published. Forensic genetic fingerprinting can be defined as the comparison of the DNA in a person's nucleated cells with that identified in biological matter found at the scene of a crime or with the DNA of another person for the purpose of identification or exclusion. The application of these techniques introduces new factual evidence to criminal investigations and court cases. However, the first case (March 1985) was not strictly a forensic case but one of immigration. The first application of DNA fingerprinting saved a young boy from deportation and the method thus captured the public's sympathy. In Alec Jeffreys' words: "If our first case had been forensic I believe it would have been challenged and the process may well have been damaged in the courts." The forensic implications of genetic fingerprinting were nevertheless obvious, and improvements of the laboratory process led already in 1987 to the very first application in a forensic case. Two teenage girls had been raped and murdered on different occasions in nearby English villages, one in 1983, and the other in 1986. Semen was obtained from each of the two crime scenes. The case was spectacular because it surprisingly excluded a suspected man, Richard Buckland, and matched another man, Colin Pitchfork, who attempted to evade the DNA dragnet by persuading a friend to give a sample on his behalf. Pitchfork confessed to committing the crimes after he was confronted with the evidence that his DNA profile matched the trace DNA from the two crime scenes. For 2 years the Lister Institute of Leicester where Jeffreys was employed was the only laboratory in the world doing this work. But it was around 1987 when companies such as Cellmark, the academic medico-legal institutions around the world, the national police, law enforcement agencies, and so on started to evaluate, improve upon, and employ the new tool. The years after the discovery of DNA fingerprinting were characterized by a mood of cooperation and interdisciplinary research. None of the many young researchers who has been there will ever forget the DNA fingerprint congresses which were held on five continents, in Bern (1990), in Belo Horizonte (1992), in Hyderabad (1994), in Melbourne (1996), and in Pt. Elizabeth (1999), and then shut down with the good feeling that the job was done. Everyone read the *Fingerprint News* distributed for free by the University of Cambridge since 1989. This affectionate little periodical published non-stylish short articles directly from the bench without impact factors and resumed networking activities in the different fields of applications. The period in the 1990s was the golden research age of DNA fingerprinting succeeded by two decades of engineering, implementation, and high-throughput application. From the Foreword of Alec Jeffreys in *Fingerprint*

News, Issue 1, January 1989: "Dear Colleagues, [...] I hope that Fingerprint News will cover all aspects of hypervariable DNA and its application, including both multi-locus and single-locus systems, new methods for studying DNA polymorphisms, the population genetics of variable loci and the statistical analysis of fingerprint data, as well as providing useful technical tips for getting good DNA profiles [...]. May your bands be variable."

Jeffreys' original technology, now obsolete for forensic use, underwent important developments in terms of the basic methodology, that is, from Southern blot to PCR, from radioactive to fluorescent labels, from slab gels to capillary electrophoresis. As the technique became more sensitive, the handling simple and automated and the statistical treatment straightforward, DNA profiling, as the method was renamed, entered the forensic routine laboratories around the world in storm. But, what counts in the Pitchfork case and what still counts today is the process to get DNA identification results accepted in legal proceedings. Spectacular fallacies, from the historical 1989 case of *People vs. Castro* in New York to the case against Knox and Sollecito in Italy (2007–2013) where literally DNA fingerprinting was on trial, disclosed severe insufficiencies in the technical protocols and especially in the DNA evidence interpretation and raised *nolens volens* doubts on the scientific and evidentiary value of forensic DNA fingerprinting. These cases are rare but frequent enough to remind each new generation of forensic analysts, researchers, or private sector employees that DNA evidence is nowadays an important part of factual evidence and needs thus intense scrutiny for all parts of the DNA analysis and interpretation process.

In the following I will briefly describe the development of DNA fingerprinting to a standardized investigative method for court use which has since 1984 led to the conviction of thousands of criminals and to the exoneration of many wrongfully suspected or convicted individuals. Genetic fingerprinting *per se* could of course not reduce the criminal rate in any of the many countries in the world, which employ this method. But DNA profiling adds hard scientific value to the evidence and strengthens thus (principally) the credibility of the legal system.

The Technological Evolution of Forensic DNA Profiling

In the classical DNA fingerprinting method radio-labeled DNA probes containing minisatellite or oligonucleotide sequences are hybridized to DNA that has been digested with a restriction enzyme, separated by agarose electrophoresis and immobilized on a membrane by Southern blotting or—in the case of the oligonucleotide probes—immobilized directly in the dried gel. The radio-labeled probe hybridizes to a set of minisatellites or oligonucleotide stretches in genomic DNA contained in restriction fragments whose size differ because of variation in the numbers of repeat units. After washing away excess probe the exposure to X-ray film (autoradiography) allows these variable fragments to be visualized, and their profiles compared between individuals. Minisatellite probes, called 33.6 and 33.15, were most widely used in the UK, most parts of Europe and the USA, whereas pentameric $(CAC)/(GTG)_5$ probes were predominantly applied in Germany. These so-called multilocus probes (MLP) detect sets of 15 to 20 variable fragments per individual ranging from 3.5 to 20 kb in size. But the multi-locus profiling method had several limitations despite its successful application to crime and kinship cases until the middle of the 1990s. Running conditions or DNA quality issues render the exact matching between bands often difficult. To overcome this, forensic laboratories adhered to binning approaches, where fixed or floating bins were defined relative to the observed DNA fragment size, and adjusted to the resolving power of the detection system. Second, fragment association within one DNA fingerprint profile is not known, leading to statistical errors due to possible linkage between loci. Third, for obtaining optimal profiles the method required substantial amounts of high molecular weight DNA and thus excludes the majority of crime-scene samples from the analysis. To overcome some of these limitations, single-locus profiling was developed. Here a single hypervariable locus is detected by a specific single-locus probe (SLP) using high stringency hybridization. Typically, four SLPs were used in a reprobing approach, yielding eight alleles of four independent loci per individual. This method requires only 10 ng of genomic DNA and has been validated through extensive experiments and forensic casework, and for many years provided a robust and valuable system for individual identification. Nevertheless, all these different restriction fragment length polymorphism (RFLP)-based methods were still limited by the available quality and quantity of the DNA and also hampered by difficulties to reliably compare genetic profiles from different sources, labs, and techniques. What was needed was a DNA code, which could ideally be generated even from a single nucleated cell and from highly degraded DNA, a code, which could be rapidly generated, numerically encrypted, automatically compared, and easily supported in court. Indeed, starting in the early 1990s DNA fingerprinting methods based on RFLP analysis were gradually supplanted by methods based on PCR because of the improved sensitivity, speed, and genotyping precision. Microsatellites, in the forensic community usually referred to short tandem repeats (STRs), were found to be ideally suited for forensic applications. STR typing is more sensitive than single-locus RFLP methods, less prone to allelic dropout than VNTR (variable number of tandem repeat) systems, and more discriminating than other PCR-based typing methods, such as HLA-DQA1. More than 2,000 publications now detail the technology, hundreds of different population groups have been studied, new technologies as, for example, the miniSTRs have been developed and standard protocols have been validated in laboratories worldwide. Forensic DNA profiling is currently performed using a panel of multi-allelic STR markers which are structurally analogous to the original minisatellites but with much shorter repeat tracts and thus easier to amplify and multiplex with PCR. Up to 30 STRs can be detected in a single capillary electrophoresis injection generating for each individual a unique genetic code. Basically there are two sets of STR markers complying with the standards requested by criminal databases around the world: the European standard set of 12 STR markers and the US CODIS standard of 13 markers. Due to partial overlap, they form together a standard of 18 STR markers in total. The incorporation of these STR markers into commercial kits has improved the application of these markers for all kinds of DNA evidence with reproducible results from as less than three nucleated cells and extracted even from severely compromised material. The probability that two individuals will have identical markers at each of 13 different STR loci within their DNA exceeds one out of a billion. If a DNA match occurs between an accused individual and a crime scene stain, the correct courtroom expression would be that the probability of a match if the crime-scene sample came from someone other than the suspect (considering the random, not closely-related man) is at most one in a billion. The uniqueness of each person's DNA (with the exception of monozygotic twins) and its simple numerical codification led to the establishment of government-controlled criminal investigation DNA databases in the developed nations around the world, the first in 1995 in the UK. When a match is made from such a DNA database to link a crime scene sample to an offender who has provided a DNA sample to a database that link is often referred to as a cold hit. A cold hit is of value as an investigative lead for the police agency to a specific suspect. China (approximately 16 million profiles, the United States (approximately 10 million profiles), and the UK (approximately 6 million profiles) maintain the largest DNA database in the world. The percentage of databased persons is on the increase in all countries with a national DNA database, but the proportions are not the same by the far: whereas in the UK about 10% of the population is in the national DNA database, the percentage in Germany and the Netherlands is only about 0.9% and 0.8%, respectively.

Lineage Markers in Forensic Analysis

Lineage markers have special applications in forensic genetics. Y chromosome analysis is very helpful in cases where there is an excess of DNA from a female victim and only a low proportion from a male perpetrator. Typical examples include sexual assault without ejaculation, sexual assault by a vasectomized male, male DNA under the fingernails of a victim, male 'touch' DNA on the skin, and the clothing or belongings of a female victim. Mitochondrial DNA (mtDNA) is of importance for the analyses of low level nuclear DNA samples, namely from unidentified (typically skeletonized) remains, hair shafts without roots, or very old specimens where only heavily degraded DNA is available. The unusual non-recombinant mode of inheritance of Y and mtDNA weakens the statistical weight of a match between individual samples but makes the method efficient for the reconstruction of the paternal or maternal relationship, for example in mass disaster investigations or in historical reconstructions. A classic case is the identification of two missing children of the Romanov family, the last Russian monarchy. MtDNA analysis combined with additional DNA testing of material from the mass grave near Yekaterinburg gave virtually irrefutable evidence that the two individuals recovered from a second grave nearby are the two missing children of the Romanov family: the Tsarevich Alexei and one of his sisters. Interestingly, a point heteroplasmy, that is, the presence of two slightly different mtDNA haplotypes within an individual, was found in the mtDNA of the Tsar and his relatives, which was in 1991 a contentious finding. In the early 1990s when the bones were first analyzed, a point heteroplasmy was believed to be an extremely rare phenomenon and was not readily explainable. Today, the existence of heteroplasmy is understood to be relatively common and large population databases can be searched for its frequency at certain positions. The mtDNA evidence in the Romanov case was underpinned by Y-STR analysis where a 17-locus haplotype from the remains of Tsar Nicholas II matched exactly to the femur of the putative Tsarevich and also to a living Romanov relative. Other studies demonstrated that very distant family branches can be traced back to common ancestors who lived hundreds of years ago. Currently forensic Y chromosome typing has gained wide acceptance with the introduction of highly sensitive panels of up to 27 STRs including rapidly mutating markers. The determination of the match probability between Y-STR or mtDNA profiles via the mostly applied counting method requires large, representative, and quality-assessed databases of haplotypes sampled in appropriate reference populations, because the multiplication of individual allele frequencies is not valid as for independently inherited autosomal STRs. Other estimators for the haplotype match probability than the count estimator have been proposed and evaluated using empirical data, however, the biostatistical interpretation remains complicated and controversial and research continues. The largest forensic Y chromosome haplotype database is the YHRD (http://www.yhrd. org) hosted at the Institute of Legal Medicine and Forensic Sciences in Berlin, Germany, with about 115,000 haplotypes sampled in 850 populations. The largest forensic mtDNA database is EMPOP (http://www.empop.org) hosted at the Institute of Legal Medicine in Innsbruck, Austria, with about 33,000 haplotypes sampled in 63 countries. More than 235 institutes have actually submitted data to the YHRD and 105 to EMPOP, a compelling demonstration of the level of networking activities between forensic science institutes around the world. That additional intelligence information is potentially derivable from such large datasets becomes obvious when a target DNA profile is searched against a collection of geographically annotated Y chromosomal or mtDNA profiles. Because linearly inherited markers have a highly non-random geographical distribution the target profile shares characteristic variants with geographical neighbors due to common ancestry. This link between genetics, genealogy, and geography could provide investigative leads for investigators in non-suspect cases as illustrated in the following case.

In 2002, a woman was found with a smashed skull and covered in blood but still alive in her Berlin apartment. Her life was saved by intensive medical care. Later she told the police that she had let a man into her apartment, and he had immediately attacked her. The man was subletting the apartment next door. The evidence collected at the scene and in the neighboring apartment included a baseball cap, two towels, and a glass. The evidence was sent to the state police laboratory in Berlin, Germany and was analyzed with conventional autosomal STR profiling. Stains on the baseball cap and on one towel revealed a pattern consistent with that of the tenant, whereas two different male DNA profiles were found on a second bath towel and on the glass. The tenant was eliminated as a suspect because he was absent at the time of the offense, but two unknown men (different in autosomal but identical in Y-STRs) who shared the apartment were suspected. Unfortunately, the apartment had been used by many individuals of both European and African nationalities, so the initial search for the two men became very difficult. The police obtained a court order for Y-STR haplotyping to gain information about the unknown men's population affiliation. Prerequisites for such biogeographic analyses are large reference databases containing Y-STR haplotypes also typed for ancestry informative single nucleotide markers (SNP) markers from hundreds of different populations. The YHRD proved useful to infer the population origin of the unknown man. The database inquiry indicated a patrilineage of Southern European ancestry, whereas an African descent was unlikely. The police were able to track down the tenant in Italy, and with his help, establish the identity of one of the unknown men, who was also Italian. When questioning this man, the police used the information retrieved from Y-STR profiling that he had shared the apartment in Berlin with a paternal relative. This relative was identified as his nephew. Because of the close-knit relationship within the family, this information would probably not have been easily retrieved from the uncle without the prior knowledge. The nephew was suspected of the attempted murder in Berlin. He was later arrested in Italy, where he had committed another violent robbery.

Information on the biogeographic origin of an unknown DNA could also be retrieved from a number of ancestry informative SNPs (AISNPs) on autosomes or insertion/deletion polymorphisms but perhaps even better from so-called mini-haplotypes with only <10 SNPs spanning small molecular intervals (<10 kb) with very low recombination among sites. Each 'minihap' behaves like a locus with multiple haplotype lineages (alleles) that have evolved from the ancestral human haplotype. All copies of each distinct haplotype are essentially identical by descent. Thus, they fall like Y and mtDNA into the lineage-informative category of genetic markers and are thus useful for connecting an individual to a family or ancestral genetic pool.

Benefits and Risks of Forensic DNA

The steady growth in the size of forensic DNA databases raises issues on the criteria of inclusion and retention and doubts on the efficiency, commensurability, and infringement of privacy of such large personal data collections. In contrast to the past, not only serious but all crimes are subject to DNA analysis generating millions and millions of DNA profiles, many of which are stored and continuously searched in national DNA databases. And as always when big datasets are gathered new mining procedures based on correlation became feasible. For example, 'Familial DNA Database Searching' is based on near matches between a crime stain and a databased person, which could be a near relative of the true perpetrator. Again the first successful familial search was conducted in UK in 2004 and led to the conviction of Craig Harman of manslaughter. Craig Harman was convicted because of partial matches from Harman's brother. The strategy was subsequently applied in some US states but is not conducted at the national level. It was during a dragnet that it first became public knowledge that the German police were also already involved in familial search strategies. In a little town in Northern Germany the police arrested a young man accused of rape because they had analyzed the DNA of his two brothers who had participated in the dragnet. Because of partial matches between crime scene DNA profiles and these brothers they had identified the suspect. In contrast to other countries, the Federal Constitutional Court of Germany decided in December 2012 against the future court use of this kind of evidence.

Civil rights and liberties are crucial for democratic societies and plans to extend forensic DNA databases to whole populations need to be condemned. Alec Jeffreys early on has questioned the way UK police collects DNA profiles, holding not only convicted individuals but also arrestees without conviction, suspects cleared in an investigation, or even innocent people never charged with an offence. He also criticized that large national databases as the NDNAD of England and Wales are likely skewed socioeconomically. It has been pointed out that most of the matches refer to minor offences; according to *GeneWatch* in Germany 63% of the database matches provided are related to theft while <3% related to rape and murder. The changes to the UK database came in the 2012's Protection of Freedoms bill, following a major defeat at the European Court of Human Rights in 2008. As of May 2013 1.1 million profiles (of about 7 million) had been destroyed to remove innocent people's profiles from the database. In 2005 the incoming government of Portugal proposed a DNA database containing samples from every Portuguese citizen. Following public objections, the government limited the database to criminals. A recent study on the public views on DNA database-related matters showed that a more critical attitude towards wider national databases is correlated with the age and education of the respondents. A deeper public awareness on the benefits and risks of very large DNA collections need to be built and common ethical and privacy standards for the development and governance of DNA databases need to be adopted where the citizen's perspectives are taken into consideration.

The Future of Forensic DNA Analysis

The forensic community, as it always has, is facing the question in which direction the DNA Fingerprint technology will be developed. A growing number of colleagues are convinced that DNA sequencing will soon replace methods based on fragment length analysis and there are good arguments for this position. With the emergence of current Next Generation Sequencing (NGS) technologies, the body of forensically useful data can potentially be expanded and analyzed quickly and cost-efficiently. Given the enormous number of potentially informative DNA loci—which of those should be sequenced? In my opinion there are four types of polymorphisms which deserve a place on the analytic device: an array of 20–30 autosomal STRs which complies with the standard sets used in the national and international databases around the world, a highly discriminating set of Y chromosomal markers, individual and signature polymorphisms in the control and coding region of the mitochondrial genome, as well as ancestry and phenotype inference SNPs. Indeed, a promising NGS approach with the simultaneous analysis of 10 STRs, 386 autosomal ancestry and phenotype informative SNPs, and the complete mtDNA genome has been presented recently. Currently, the rather high error rates are preventing NGS technologies from being used in forensic routine, but it is foreseeable that the technology will be improved in terms of accuracy and reliability. Time is another essential factor in police investigations which will be considerably reduced in future applications of DNA profiling. Commercial instruments capable of producing a database-compatible DNA profile within 2 hours exist and are currently under validation for law enforcement use. The hands-free 'swab in—profile out' process consists of automated extraction, amplification, separation, detection, and allele calling without human intervention. In the US the promise of on-site DNA analysis has already altered the way in which DNA could be collected in future. In a recent decision the Supreme Court of the United States held that 'when officers make an arrest supported by probable cause to hold for a serious offense and bring the suspect to the station to be detained in custody, taking and analyzing a cheek swab of the arrestee's DNA is, like fingerprinting and photographing, a legitimate police booking procedure' (*Maryland v. Alonzo Jay King, Jr.*). In other words, DNA can be taken from any arrestee, rightly or wrongly arrested, as a part of the normal booking procedure. Twenty-eight states and the federal government now take DNA swabs after arrests with the aim of comparing profiles to the CODIS database, creating links to unsolved cases and to identify the person (Associated Press, 3 June 2013). Driven by the rapid technological progress DNA actually becomes another metric of quick identification. It remains to be seen whether rapid DNA technologies will alter the way in which DNA is collected by police in other countries. In Germany for example the DNA collection is still regulated by the code of the criminal procedure and the use of DNA profiling for identification purposes only is excluded. Because national legislations are basically so different, a worldwide system to interrogate DNA profiles from criminal justice databases seems currently a very distant project.

At present the forensic DNA technology directly affects the lives of millions people worldwide. The general acceptance of this technique is still high, reports on the DNA identification of victims of the 9/11 terrorist attacks, of natural disasters as the Hurricane Katrina, and of recent wars (for example, in former Yugoslavia) and dictatorship (for example, in Argentina) impress the public in the same way as police investigators in white suits securing DNA evidence at a broken door. CSI watchers know, and even professionals believe, that DNA will inevitably solve the case just following the motto *Do Not Ask, it's DNA, stupid!* But the affirmative view changes and critical questions are raised. It should not be assumed that the benefits of forensic DNA fingerprinting will necessarily override the social and ethical costs.

This short article leaves many of such questions unanswered. Alfred Nobel used his fortune to institute a prize for work "in ideal direction." What would be the ideal direction in which DNA fingerprinting, one of the great discoveries in recent history, should be developed?

6

False Confessions Can Be a Cause of Wrongful Conviction

Elaine Cassel

Elaine Cassel is a professor of law at Concord University School of Law in Virginia. She is also an attorney, a freelance writer, and the author of Criminal Behavior.

Most would agree that criminals must be prosecuted, and if proven guilty they must experience some sort of punishment. But what if they are wrongfully convicted because of an untrue confession? An admission of guilt or confession is seen as incontrovertible by the justice system. But documented cases have proven that confessions are often obtained through inappropriate measures, and that these confessions can be wrong or false. This viewpoint explores various reasons why false confessions occur and offers suggestions on how to eliminate the conditions that lead to these acts of injustice.

On December 5 of this year, the Manhattan district attorney's office made a rare move: It asked a judge to dismiss all charges against five men it had earlier prosecuted.

As teenagers, the men had been convicted and incarcerated for raping a jogger in Central Park in 1989, and they had since served years of jail time for the crimes. Now, however, the actual perpetrator, an older man named Matias Reyes, has been linked

"The False Confessions in the Central Park Jogger Case," by Elaine Cassel, CounterPunch, December 21, 2002. Reprinted by permission.

to the victim with DNA evidence–after confessing to the rape and assault earlier this year.

What went wrong, and why? Why were the boys convicted in the first place? There is plenty of blame to go around. But their false confessions played a large role, and the circumstances of how those confessions came about are worth a long, close look.

The Jogger Case and Its Miscarriage of Justice

In April 1989, in New York City, violent crime rates—murders, rapes, and robberies—were out of control, and people were afraid to walk city streets. The Central Park jogger case set a record (and served as a symbol) for brutality—it was a violent rape in which the victim was also badly beaten, leading to a lengthy hospitalization.

Five teenagers, ranging in age from 14 to 16 years, who had been implicated in a separate series of muggings, were questioned about the rape. The boys were black; the victim was white. Some say that things began to go wrong right there—that the race factor trumped a search for the truth. The idea of a roving gang of black boys brutally beating and raping a white woman fit the schema of the public's fear of African-Americans and of teenage gangs.

All of the boys made statements to the police, though not one of them admitted to actually having intercourse with the victim. The search for the perpetrator stopped.

Meanwhile, the real perpetrator, Reyes—who had committed a rape a few days before the jogger's, and would go on to rape and kill—remained out there. Even at the time, it was clear that his modus operandi matched the assault and rape of the jogger, but prosecutors did not follow leads relating to Reyes.

Why, when no physical evidence linked the five boys to the crime and their confessions were implausible and mutually contradictory, were the boys convicted?

In part, because a defendant's confession is considered by judges and juries to be compelling and unequivocal evidence. Indeed, the power of a confession is so strong, according to

McCormick's treatise on evidence, as to make other aspects of the trial superfluous. As demonstrated in this case, a confession can even override strong physical evidence to the contrary.

Moreover, at the same time that confessions are viewed as virtually incontrovertible, police are allowed to use a number of wrongful tactics to get them. These tactics greatly increase the possibility of false confessions, and go a long way towards explaining why they occur.

Some Current, Psychologically Coercive Interrogation Tactics Should Not Be Permitted

The Supreme Court limits the admissibility of confessions that are coerced or given without the requisite Miranda warnings. But what counts as coercion?

Torture and beatings are obviously coercive, and were ruled to be so as early as 1936 in *Brown v. Mississippi*. Fortunately, they are largely a thing of the past. (However, in the past couple of years there has been a resurgence of reported violence perpetrated during interrogations in New York City, Los Angeles, and Prince Georges' County, Maryland).

In contrast, psychological coercion, under current rules, does not automatically count as coercion; rather, psychological tactics must be proven to be coercive under a "totality of circumstances" test, as the Supreme Court held in *Haynes v. Washington*.

As a result, officers are indoctrinated into the psychological methods of interrogation designed to get a suspect to confess. Manuals tell investigators, for instance, to use the physical environment to law enforcement advantage, by creating small, starkly furnished, and brightly lit interrogation rooms; they instruct in how to get in a defendant's face and invade his personal space. Officers learn how to conduct long interviews that may span three or four days, with little respect for a suspect's need for sleep, food, or bathroom breaks.

The purpose of all these tactics, of course, to break down recalcitrant suspects. The problem is that they tend to break down vulnerable and innocent people as well as—or perhaps even better than—the hardened and guilty recidivist.

Deceptive Tactics, in Particular, Often Induce False Confessions

Deceptive tactics are also encouraged. Investigators are taught to minimize the likely results of suspects' confessions, and to suggest to suspects that they will get a better "deal" if they talk than if they remain silent. They pretend to identify with the suspects and to offer "rationalizations" for suspects' alleged crimes, suggesting the crimes were not so bad, and thus confessing them wouldn't be so bad, either.

Interrogators are allowed to tell suspects that if they take a polygraph and "pass," they will be released—which is not always the case. Then, once the polygraph has been taken, investigators may lie about its results if they think that would be helpful—telling a defendant falsely that he failed.

Consider, for instance, the case of an Egyptian man who was wrongfully charged with lying to the FBI in post-September 11 investigations. He falsely confessed because he was told he had "failed" a polygraph, and that if he did not confess, the government would make life for his family in Egypt "hell." His conviction has been overturned, but not until he served 31 days in solitary confinement.

Similarly, interrogators are encouraged to falsely tell suspects they believe them to be guilty, and that another suspect or physical evidence has implicated them. That was what happened in the Central Park jogger case: The boys were told that hairs linked them to the victim's body, which turned out not to be true.

These lies can be very harmful, since the suspect can, through repetition, be induced by the investigator to believe them. Studies show that some people who falsely confess do so because they internalize the repeated suggestions and scenarios of questioners. Nevertheless, offering scenarios for the suspect to buy into, is still a common tactic of investigators.

Indeed, a popular text of investigative techniques explains how to offer alternative explanations for how and why a crime occurred, and encourage the subject to pick "a," "b," or "c." Once the subject makes his choice, the questioner is told to help the subject "fill in the blanks," often falsely.

A case in point is the infamous false confession of Paul Ingram, a highly suggestible person who confessed to totally incredible allegations of ritualistic sexual abuse against his daughters (subsequently proved to be totally false). Ingram is still serving out a 25-year sentence, because he confessed.

Accusation after accusation was thrown at Ingram, with the encouragement to "think about it," even "pray over it," and refresh his memory. He did even more—"confessing" to bizarre, baseless details.

Amazingly, as long as deceptive tactics like these are not deemed by a court to be coercive under the totality of the circumstances, the confessions they induce remain admissible. This is true even though statistics show that false confessions are second only to false eyewitness identification in being responsible for wrongful convictions.

Other Factors that Were at Work in the Central Park Jogger Case Interrogation

Manhattan District Attorney Robert Morgenthau's report supporting reversal of the convictions reveals other troubling aspect of the five suspects' confessions—besides investigator's lies that physical evidence linked the boys to the victim's body.

First, none of the boys admitted actually raping (that is, penetrating) the victim. Second, their tales of time and location of the rape were inconsistent not only with each other, but with statements of reliable witnesses.

Third, the suspects' conflicting and confusing statements, taken together, made no sense. It seemed, the report notes, as if the boys were talking about different crimes. It also seemed that each expected that talking would enhance his chances of become a witness against others, not a defendant in his own case.

Thus, each of the suspects' statements minimized their own involvement, while placing more blame on one or more of their buddies. Together, however, the statements (though contradictory) were taken by prosecutors, at the time, to amount to a sort of group confession. They were seen that way even though some of the boys refused to admit any guilt on their own part. (Ironically, they served longer sentences as a result of insisting on their innocence).

Playing suspects off against one another, like the other psychologically coercive tactics noted above, is entirely legal, even though it also predictably leads to false confessions. Research shows that some people will say whatever a questioner wants to hear, in order to improve their status at the expense of their partner in crime.

Investigators take advantage of this psychological fact (known as "The Prisoner's Dilemma"); they split up and during breaks, caucus with each other and returned to their suspects armed with information gained from the other. And they may begin plea-bargaining early—suggesting suspects should confess to one crime in exchange for not having to face more serious charges.

Meanwhile, that teens—some of them young teens—were involved heightened the coercive environment of the interrogation. The younger boys may not fully have understood the Miranda warnings. Behavioral science research has shown that teenagers (and many adults) generally don't; they may not understand what is meant by "waiver," and despite the warnings' language, most persist in thinking they will get to go home if they simply cooperate with the authorities.

In addition, teenagers—especially antisocial kids like these—are also egocentric and like to put themselves into the stories they tell (as I discussed in a column about the youthful sniper suspect, John Lee Malvo). At times, they lie; often, they exaggerate. A boy who ran away from the scene, for instance, might not admit it since his flight would not seem macho or manly.

Here, one of the teens also seemed to display borderline mental retardation and perhaps a psychotic mental disorder. In some of his statements, he referred to flying around the park in a blue bus. People with mental retardation are much more likely to tell any questioner what he or she wants to hear, and people who are delusional are too far out of touch with reality, of course, to make reliable statements.

Despite all these problems, the prosecutors—eager for a conviction—still went forward.

How To Stop It From Happening Again

How can we stop other cases like this from occurring? A number of simple measures could prevent many false confessions like these.

First, children, teenagers, and people with mental deficiencies should not be questioned outside the presence of a competent guardian or legal representative. In this case, none of the boys' parents were present when their children made the most damaging statements against their interests.

Second, all interrogations ought to be videotaped. In this case, the taping did not begin until after the boys had been questioned for hours. As a result, the film shows only the statements, not the psychological and environmental pressures that preceded them. Jurors could certainly get a false impression of the "confessions," viewing them outside the context of law enforcement tactics.

Third, all statements offered as confessions should not be admissible unless they are corroborated by credible and, when possible, physical evidence. Fortunately, most states do have laws that require corroboration of admissions. Unfortunately, the qualitative standard for how good the corroboration must be is quite low. Circumstantial evidence may suffice. Worse, even the statement of an accomplice, as in the Central Park jogger case, is deemed to be enough—despite the accomplice's obvious incentive to escape responsibility by placing the lion's share of blame on someone else.

Fourth, there should be strict, carefully-enforced time limits on interrogations. Questioning that goes beyond three or four hours begins to be coercive; questioners intensify their techniques, and subjects become fatigued, confused, even disoriented. In the jogger case, the interrogations—which ranged from fourteen to thirty hours—clearly crossed the line from questioning into coercion.

Fifth, contrary to current Supreme Court standards, law enforcement lies to suspects should be forbidden. As noted above, the "confessions" such lies prompt are often highly unreliable.

Sixth, and finally, prosecutors should be held to their duty to do justice. Because they are immune from suit, they are unaccountable—except to voters—for negligence and fraud. Requiring them to vouch for the evidence produced by their investigators and law enforcement, might make them think twice about putting on any evidence and hoping it sticks.

Defense attorneys can lose their licenses for putting on false and misleading evidence, even though their duty is to defend zealously. Prosecutors, on the other hand, often do so with impunity, even though their duty is to serve justice, not to convict. That needs to stop. Prosecutors should be held as closely accountable for what they do as are defense attorneys.

The Cost of False Confessions

Some observers have expressed little sympathy for the falsely convicted boys, who seem to have been muggers, even if they were not rapists. But of course, a mugging is a world away from a rape, for which they were incarcerated. And more fundamentally, the Constitution guarantees that the punishment fit the crime—not some other, worse crime one did not commit.

In any case, one need not have an excess of sympathy for the boys in order to condemn the injustice done here. One need only have sympathy for the next woman whom the real perpetrator, Reyes, went on to rape and murder, and for the jogger-victim, who did not get justice for 13 years.

They deserved much better. So did the boys, and so do we all.

7

Research Suggests Many Are Susceptible to Giving False Confessions

Margaret Weigel and John Wihbey

Margaret Weigel is a senior marketing manager at LEGO Education. She previously served as a site strategist, editor, and education content developer for Harvard Kennedy School's Journalist's Resource. *John Wihbey is an assistant professor of journalism and the head of graduate programs in the School of Journalism at Northeastern University in Boston, Massachusetts.*

This viewpoint examines recent research on exonerations and false confessions. The findings suggest that the vast majority of false confessions are for homicide cases, which generally result in some of the most severe sentences. Additionally, false confessions are a major source of wrongful convictions among those sentenced under the age of eighteen. The research suggests that interrogation techniques and the physiological effects they have on the accused can cause false confessions, suggesting that confessions should be given less weight as evidence in trials and interrogation techniques should be reevaluated.

Researchers have been increasingly focusing on the science behind interrogation techniques and confessions—and emerging criminal justice system data patterns—with the hope of better understanding how false confessions are produced and how to limit the chances innocent persons are imprisoned.

The topic of false confessions has again come into the public eye as the University of Michigan and Northwestern University law schools continue to compile data as part of the new National Registry of Exonerations. Scholars with that project note in a 2013 report: "For homicide exonerations, the leading cause of false conviction is perjury or false accusations, mostly deliberate misidentifications. Homicide cases also include a high rate of official misconduct, and 74% of all false confessions in the database."

As the *Wall Street Journal* noted in a Sept. 8, 2013 report, National Registry of Exonerations statistics suggest that young people in particular are more prone to admitting guilt for crimes they did not commit. "Thirty-eight percent of exonerations for crimes allegedly committed by youth under 18 in the last quarter century involved false confessions," reporter Zusha Eilson writes, "compared with 11% for adults, according to a new database of 1,155 individuals who were wrongly convicted and later cleared of all charges." Indeed, in California, which faces severe prison overcrowding issues, there has been debate about new policies that specifically address the issue of coerced confessions by young people.

Data produced through experiments are also providing new insights. For example, a 2013 study published in *Law and Human Behavior*, "Innocence and Resisting Confession During Interrogation: Effects on Physiologic Activity," performs experiments on innocent subjects to look at the biological realities of being questioned and how stress affects those being interrogated. The findings "suggest that innocent suspects underestimate the threat of interrogation and that resisting pressures to confess can diminish suspects' physiologic resources and lead to false confessions."

The study's authors—Max Guyll, Stephanie Madon, Yueran Yang, and Daniel G. Lannin of Iowa State University, Kyle Scherr of

Central Michigan University, and Sarah Greathouse of the RAND Corporation—also conclude:

> *The current findings show that the state of being actually innocent produces an immediate and fundamental difference in suspects that could set in motion an array of ill-advised decisions and behaviors that could put innocent suspects' long-term outcomes in jeopardy. It should be noted that the initial physiologic differences associated with innocence and guilt are not necessarily important in and of themselves, but rather are significant because they reflect critical initial differences between the innocent and the guilty in how they differently construe the same situation. The smaller physiologic reactions of the innocent occurring in response to being accused and interrogated signal the experience of less stress, indicating that they perceive themselves to be at less risk—a perception that would discourage taking strong self-protective actions, such as invoking one's rights to silence and counsel.*

Conventional wisdom maintains that the "bluff"—an interrogation technique in which investigators state they have potentially damning evidence but do not claim that this evidence implicates the accused—is of little concern to the innocent falsely accused but can frighten the guilty into confessing. According to The Innocence Project, however, approximately 25% of convicted criminals ultimately exonerated had, in fact, confessed to the crime, as the *Economist* notes. A 2015 study published in *Psychological Science* finds evidence that, under lab conditions:

> *[P]eople can come to visualize and recall detailed false memories of engaging in criminal behavior. Not only could the young adults in our sample be led to generate such memories, but their rate of false recollection was high, and the memories themselves were richly detailed. Additionally, false memories for perpetrating crime showed signs that they may have been generated in a way that is similar to the way in which false memories for noncriminal emotional memories are generated. False memories for committing crime also shared many characteristics with true memories.*

A 2011 study published in *Law and Human Behavior*, "Inside Interrogation: The Lie, the Bluff and False Confessions," describes a series of laboratory experiments that test how the bluff technique correlates with confessions gained from innocent parties. Subjects were instructed to complete a task, then were falsely accused of a transgression such as crashing the computer or collaborating with a colleague to improve their task performance. The experiment introduced variables such as bluff evidence, false evidence and less-than-honest eyewitnesses to identify which were the most likely to prompt a confession. The study was conducted by Jennifer T. Perillo and Saul M. Kassin of CUNY's John Jay College of Criminal Justice.

Key study highlights include:

- In the first test group, 43 of 71 subjects confessed to the experimenter that they had pressed a computer key they had been instructed to avoid when, in fact, they had not; an additional 10% admitted to pressing the key to a study observer. A second group that tested subject reactions to charges of cheating produced nearly identical percentages of false confessions.

- In the first test group, "introduction of an innocence-affirming witness did not bluff participants from the accusations and pressures of the situation."

- In the second test group, "94% of participants expressed some degree of certainty in their own innocence: 24 (73%) were completely certain, 7 (21%) were somewhat to mostly certain; 2 (6%) said they were somewhat certain of their guilt. Despite the fact that most participants knew they were innocent, however, a majority agreed to confess."

- In the second test group, "75% of those who confessed in the bluff condition explicitly cited the bluff as the reason for that decision." Reasons cited for the confession included wanting to finish the study and feeling sorry for the experimenter.

- Ninety percent of subjects who believed that a hidden camera had captured their actions confessed, while only twenty-seven percent of control subjects did.

The study's authors note that "innocent people who stand accused believe that their innocence will become apparent to others … which leads them to waive their *Miranda* right to silence and to an attorney." However, they conclude that these experiments "convincingly demonstrate that use of the bluff tactic in an interrogation can induce compliant false confessions from innocent people. Importantly, however, additional research is needed to reassess the predicted effectiveness of the bluff on the true confession rates of perpetrators."

8

How Can Wrongful Convictions Be Overturned?

David Hamer and Gary Edmond

David Hamer is a professor of evidence law at the University of Sydney, and Gary Edmond is a professor of law at the University of New South Wales.

Sometimes people are wrongfully convicted of a crime, and later when their cases are appealed because of additional evidence to the contrary—especially DNA evidence—they are proven to be innocent. But in Australia this process could potentially be thwarted. In New South Wales, Australia, the government believes that wrongful convictions simply do not occur in the first place. They insist that the trial procedure whereby twelve jurors find a person guilty is generally very accurate, and the entire process of presenting new evidence via appeals should not occur, as it is at the expense of the government.

A person is wrongly convicted of a serious crime, then fresh evidence reveals they are, in fact, innocent. It's a thriller movie formula and you'd hope that if this were to happen, justice would prevail.

A bill introduced to the New South Wales parliament earlier this month, however, jeopardises this very process. It aims to abolish the DNA Review Panel, which is empowered to arrange fresh DNA analysis of defendants convicted of very serious crimes who claim to be innocent. The panel could then refer cases back to the Court of Criminal Appeal (CCA). Currently, the bill abolishing the panel looks likely to pass.

The DNA Review Panel should be replaced with a Criminal Cases Review Commission (CCRC) with the powers and resources to effectively uncover wrongful convictions.

During its six-and-a-half years of operation, the panel received about 30 applications, but made no referrals to the CCA. The NSW government has taken this as a sign that wrongful convictions simply don't occur in NSW. But this is a dubious conclusion; inevitably, errors are made.

It's true that relatively few wrongful convictions are discovered in Australia—Lindy Chamberlain, the Mickelberg brothers and Andrew Mallard are a few rare examples. But this shouldn't be taken to mean that Australian criminal justice makes few mistakes. The reason few errors are discovered is that it's so hard to identify them.

A criminal conviction is very difficult to dislodge. At trial, the defendant is presumed innocent. But the appeal court will presume the convicted defendant to be guilty, and therefore be reluctant to overturn the jury verdict.

There is an assumption that the jury of 12 is better suited to fact-finding than a bench of three or five appeal court judges. It would be undemocratic for the appeal court to intrude upon the domain of the jury—the "constitutional fact-finder" —and the appeal court will also be reluctant to give encouragement to appeals, and create too much work for itself.

After appeal, it is even harder to overturn a wrongful conviction. Traditionally, the defendant may petition the Crown for mercy or a referral back to the appeal court. However, this is not a task the government is well suited for, as political considerations inevitably intrude.

Consider the ongoing Tasmanian case of Susan Neill-Fraser, convicted for the murder of her husband and the subject of the documentary Shadow of Doubt. The film makes a strong case that the evidence against Neill-Fraser was severely flawed, and that there are other highly plausible explanations for what may have happened to Neill-Fraser's husband.

And yet, even though Neill-Fraser is educated, articulate, well-resourced, and has the assistance of family and supporters, she still cannot get the Tasmanian government to refer the case back to the appeal court.

In recent decades, some jurisdictions have established alternative post-appeal mechanisms. England, Scotland and Norway have Criminal Cases Review Commissions. NSW has its DNA Review Panel. And South Australia recently introduced a further appeal on the basis of "fresh and compelling evidence." But in NSW at least, the eligibility requirements for application to the Panel are exceedingly narrow. Defendants could only apply if they had been convicted of the most serious offences, and their conviction was prior to September 19, 2006.

Further, the defendant must specify the biological material for testing. How is an innocent defendant supposed to know enough about the crime and the investigation to be able to satisfy this requirement? Of course, relatively few crimes other than sexual assaults and crimes of violence where identity is in issue would generate useful DNA evidence, let alone evidence that had been gathered and preserved. So it's not surprising the DNA Review Panel achieved nothing.

In NSW, wrongfully convicted defendants may also seek to get their cases back before the CCA, by application to the Supreme Court. But the Supreme Court has indicated that it will require something pretty extraordinary to make a referral. As the Supreme Court told serial killer Ivan Milat, it:

> ...is not intended to provide a convicted person with yet another avenue of appeal after the usual avenues have been exhausted.

A dozen convictions were overturned on subsequent appeal in the first years of the 21st century in Australia, but these were virtually all cases of police corruption uncovered by the Wood

Royal Commission. Other than that, referrals to the appeal court and quashed convictions are extremely rare.

Besides police corruption, there are many other causes of wrongful conviction: biased or incompetent experts, prosecutorial misconduct, lying witnesses, mistaken eyewitnesses, ineffective defence counsel. But there is no mechanism for investigating these possible causes. The burden is placed on the defendant to do the work, yet how is the defendant, in prison, without resources or skills, meant to carry this burden?

This is why the new South Australian appeal provision, established in May 2013, is unlikely to achieve anything. It has been wrongly described as a new "right of appeal"; but there is no right. The appeal court's permission is required, and the court can only give permission if it thinks there is "fresh and compelling evidence" of innocence.

How is a wrongfully convicted defendant, in prison and with few resources or skills, going to discharge this burden? The South Australian parliament patted itself on the back for this reform, quoting a letter from former High Court Justice Michael Kirby, who described it as:

> ...an instance of...principle triumphing over complacency and mere pragmatism.

But it is difficult to see this reform giving much hope to the wrongfully convicted.

The new South Australian law came out of independent MP Ann Bressington's bill to establish a CCRC. The state government rejected it, and South Australian attorney-general John Rau claimed:

> South Australia is not Texas. This state is not awash with wrongful convictions and the falsely imprisoned.

But since the original bill proposed an English-style CCRC, England would have provided a better comparison. With the establishment of the English CCRC, the quashing of convictions jumped from four or five a year to 20 or 30. The reason for the increase is that the CCRC is equipped with the resources and powers to investigate potential wrongful convictions.

Previously, many wrongful convictions remained hidden, just as they are in Australia today. And the English CCRC has the respect of the Court of Appeal, and is perceived by the British government as good value for money. Earlier this year, it passed its Triennial Review and received a budget increase.

Australian governments should stop pretending wrongful convictions don't happen here. Instead, they should recognise that they are an inevitable byproduct of criminal justice, and set in place an effective and fair mechanism to deal with them.

9

The Death Sentence and Wrongful Conviction

Samuel R. Gross, Barbara O'Brien, Chen Hu, and
Edward H. Kennedy

*Samuel R. Gross is associated with the University of Michigan
Law School. Barbara O'Brien is affiliated with the Michigan State
University College of Law. Chen Hu is affiliated with the American
College of Radiology Clinical Research Center. Edward H. Kennedy
is associated with the University of Pennsylvania Medical School's
department of biostatistics and epidemiology.*

*How often do innocent people get wrongfully convicted? Some assert
that this is unknowable. What is known is that in the past few
decades there has been a flood of exonerations. Prominent people in
the US justice system say they believe the rate of wrongful conviction
is low, but is this true? Researchers contend that in order to make
such claims, data are needed to prove this assertion, and that kind
of data is not available because a high concentration of exonerated
individuals are those facing the death penalty, which only account
for a very small percentage of criminal cases. In most criminal cases,
there is no follow-up or effort made to seek exoneration.*

The rate of erroneous conviction of innocent criminal
defendants is often described as not merely unknown but
unknowable. There is no systematic method to determine the
accuracy of a criminal conviction; if there were, these errors

"Rate of False Conviction of Criminal Defendants Who Are Sentenced to Death," by
Samuel R. Gross, Barbara O'Brien, Chen Hu, and Edward H. Kennedy, Proceedings of the
National Academy of Sciences, April 28, 2014. Reprinted by permission.

would not occur in the first place. As a result, very few false convictions are ever discovered, and those that are discovered are not representative of the group as a whole. In the United States, however, a high proportion of false convictions that do come to light and produce exonerations are concentrated among the tiny minority of cases in which defendants are sentenced to death. This makes it possible to use data on death row exonerations to estimate the overall rate of false conviction among death sentences. The high rate of exoneration among death-sentenced defendants appears to be driven by the threat of execution, but most death-sentenced defendants are removed from death row and resentenced to life imprisonment, after which the likelihood of exoneration drops sharply. We use survival analysis to model this effect, and estimate that if all death-sentenced defendants remained under sentence of death indefinitely, at least 4.1% would be exonerated. We conclude that this is a conservative estimate of the proportion of false conviction among death sentences in the United States.

In the past few decades a surge of hundreds of exonerations of innocent criminal defendants has drawn attention to the problem of erroneous conviction, and led to a spate of reforms in criminal investigation and adjudication. All the same, the most basic empirical question about false convictions remains unanswered: How common are these miscarriages of justice?

False convictions, by definition, are unobserved when they occur: If we know that a defendant is innocent, he is not convicted in the first place. They are also extremely difficult to detect after the fact. As a result, the great majority of innocent defendants remain undetected. The rate of such errors is often described as a "dark figure"—an important measure of the performance of the criminal justice system that is not merely unknown but unknowable.

However, there is no shortage of lawyers and judges who assert confidently that the number of false convictions is negligible. Judge Learned Hand said so in 1923: "Our [criminal] procedure has always been haunted by the ghost of the innocent man convicted. It is an unreal dream." And in 2007, Justice Antonin Scalia wrote in a concurring opinion in the Supreme Court that American criminal convictions have an "error rate of [0].027 percent—or, to put it another way, a success rate of 99.973 percent." This would be comforting, if true. In fact, the claim is silly. Scalia's ratio is derived by taking the number of known exonerations at the time, which were limited almost entirely to a small subset of murder and rape cases, using it as a measure of all false convictions (known and unknown), and dividing it by the number of all felony convictions for all crimes, from drug possession and burglary to car theft and income tax evasion.

To actually estimate the proportion of erroneous convictions we need a well-defined group of criminal convictions within which we identify all mistaken convictions, or at least most. It is hard to imagine how that could be done for criminal convictions generally, but it might be possible for capital murder.

The rate of exonerations among death sentences in the United States is far higher than for any other category of criminal convictions. Death sentences represent less than one-tenth of 1% of prison sentences in the United States, but they accounted for about 12% of known exonerations of innocent defendants from 1989 through early 2012, a disproportion of more than 130 to 1. A major reason for this extraordinary exoneration rate is that far more attention and resources are devoted to death penalty cases than to other criminal prosecutions, before and after conviction.

The vast majority of criminal convictions are not candidates for exoneration because no one makes any effort to reconsider the guilt of the defendants. Approximately 95% of felony convictions in the United States are based on negotiated pleas of guilty (plea bargains) that are entered in routine proceedings at which no evidence is presented. Few are ever subject to any review whatsoever. Most convicted defendants are never represented by an attorney after conviction, and the appeals that do take place are usually perfunctory and unrelated to guilt or innocence.

Death sentences are different. Almost all are based on convictions after jury trial, and even the handful of capital defendants who plead guilty are then subject to trial-like-sentencing hearings, usually before juries. All death sentences are reviewed on appeal; almost all are reviewed repeatedly. With few exceptions, capital defendants have lawyers as long as they remain on death row. Everyone, from the first officer on the scene of a potentially capital crime to the Chief Justice of the United States, takes capital cases more seriously than other criminal prosecutions—and knows that everybody else will do so as well. And everyone from defense lawyers to innocence projects to governors and state and federal judges is likely to be particularly careful to avoid the execution of innocent defendants.

This extraordinary difference in resources and attention generates two related effects. (*i*) Advocates for a defendant are much more likely to pursue any plausible postconviction claim of innocence if the defendant is under sentence of death. (*ii*) Courts (and other government actors) are much more likely to consider and grant such a claim if the defendant is at risk for execution. As a result, false convictions are far more likely to be detected among those cases that end in death sentences than in any other category of criminal convictions.

The high exoneration rate for death sentences suggests that a substantial proportion of innocent defendants who are sentenced to death are ultimately exonerated, perhaps a majority. If so, we can use capital exonerations as a basis for estimating a lower bound for the false conviction rate among death sentences.

Since 1973, when the first death penalty laws now in effect in the United States were enacted, 143 death-sentenced defendants have been exonerated, from 1 to 33 y after conviction (mean = 10.1 y). In a previous study we found that 2.3% of all death sentences imposed from 1973 through 1989 resulted in exoneration by the end of 2004. A study by Risinger estimated that had biological samples been available for testing in all cases, 3.3% of defendants sentenced to death between 1982 and 1989 for murders that included rape would have been exonerated by DNA evidence through February 2006. That estimate, however, is based on a small number of exonerations ($n = 11$). Both studies were limited to convictions that occurred 15 y or more before the study date, and so include a high proportion of all exonerations that will ever occur in the relevant groups. Nonetheless both studies underestimate the false conviction rate for death-sentenced defendants because they do not reflect exonerations that occur after the study period, and do not include false convictions that are never detected at all.

Capital defendants who are removed from death row but not exonerated—typically because their sentences are reduced to life imprisonment—no longer receive the extraordinary level of attention that is devoted to death row inmates. (This applies as well to those who are executed or die on death row from other causes.) If they are in fact innocent, they are much less likely to be exonerated than if they had remained on death row. As a result, the proportion of death-sentenced inmates who are exonerated understates the rate of false convictions among death sentences because the intensive search for possible errors is largely abandoned once the threat of execution is removed.

In other words, the engine that produces an exoneration rate that is a plausible proxy for the rate of false conviction among death-sentenced prisoners is the process of reinvestigation and reconsideration under threat of execution. Over time, most death-sentenced inmates are removed from death row and resentenced to life in prison—at which point their chances of exoneration appear to drop back to the background rate for all murders, or close to it. Thus, we will get a better estimate of the rate of false capital convictions if are able to estimate "what the rate of capital exonerations would be if all death sentences were subject for an indefinite period to the level of scrutiny that applies to those facing the prospect of execution." This study does just that.

Current Study

Data

We examine exonerations among defendants sentenced to death from the beginning of the "modern" death penalty in the United

States in 1973, after the Supreme Court invalidated all prior death sentencing laws, through the end of 2004. Our data come from two sources. (*i*) Death sentences since 1973 are tracked by the Bureau of Justice Statistics (BJS) of the Department of Justice, which maintains data on the current status of all death-sentenced defendants in that period. We know that 7,482 defendants were sentenced to death in the United States from January 1973 through December 2004, and we know when (if ever) each defendant was removed from death row by execution, death by other means, or legal action by courts or executive officials. (*ii*) The Death Penalty Information Center maintains a list of defendants who were sentenced to death in the United States and exonerated since the beginning of 1973, including 117 who were sentenced to death after January 1, 1973 and exonerated by legal proceedings that began before the end of 2004. We collected additional data on these cases from public records and media sources, expanding on the dataset used by Gross and O'Brien. We were able to match on several key variables 108 of the 117 death sentence exonerations in this period to specific cases in the BJS database to produce the database we analyzed.

On data collected on the status of 7,482 death-sentenced defendants as of December 31, 2004, the last day of our study, 12.6% of these defendants had been executed, 1.6% were exonerated, 4% died of suicide or natural causes while on death row, 46.1% remained on death row, and 35.8% were removed from death row but remained in prison after their capital sentences or the underlying convictions were reversed or modified.

The data is a snapshot of the status of these defendants at the end of the study period. (It would look quite different if it displayed the status of death-sentenced defendants at the end of 1985, for example, or 2000.) It cannot be used directly to estimate the rate of exoneration because exonerations are a function of time. Many of the defendants on death row at the end of 2004 had only been there for a year or two, far less than the mean of 10.1 y from conviction to exoneration for all capital exonerations since 1973.

Over time, many of those who remained on death row at the end of 2004 will be removed (or already have been); most will end up with sentences of life imprisonment. If the pattern for death sentences from 1973 through 1995 holds, over two-thirds of prisoners sentenced to death will have the judgments against them overturned. The majority will remain in prison for life, but some will be exonerated and released.

Threat of Execution

A central variable of interest is whether an exoneration took place while the defendant was still under threat of execution. The status of the defendant as under threat is obvious when a defendant is exonerated and released directly from death row. On the other side, a defendant is clearly not under threat of execution when the exoneration is the product of a process that began years after removal from death row.

In other cases, determining the threat status of the defendant at the time of exoneration is more demanding. We identify defendants who were under threat of execution to focus on exonerations that benefited from the extraordinary levels of effort and scrutiny that are applied to defendants who might be put to death. Many defendants who leave death row might be sent back. Hence the under-threat-of-execution category includes defendants who were removed from death row but remained eligible for resentencing to death, and in whose cases the prosecution was actively pursuing a new death sentence or considering whether to do so. For example, Ronald Williamson was sentenced to death in Oklahoma in 1988, and awarded a new trial in 1997 because of constitutionally inadequate representation by his trial lawyer. He was exonerated by DNA testing 2 y later, in 1999, while awaiting a retrial at which he might have been sentenced to death again. His exoneration was under threat of execution.

We also count an exoneration as under threat if the process that ultimately led to the exoneration began while the defendant was on death row, even if the final decision to release the defendant was made after he left death row. This sort of delay is common for defendants who are removed from death row when their convictions are reversed by reviewing courts but not released until months or years later when the prosecution decides to dismiss the charges. In some cases the process is more elaborate. For instance, John Thompson was sentenced to death in Louisiana in 1985. In 2001 he sought a new trial based on newly discovered evidence, but received only a reduction in his sentence to life imprisonment. Thompson successfully appealed the denial of a new trial and was acquitted in 2003. Thus, although his death sentence was vacated 2 y before his acquittal, we treat him as exonerated under threat of execution because the legal proceedings that led to exoneration began while he was on death row and ran to their conclusion two years later.

We define an exoneration under threat of execution as an exoneration that is the result of legal proceedings that were initiated while the defendant was on death row. The date we assign to an exoneration is the date of removal from death row, the last date on which the exoneration can be initiated and still count as under threat, not the date on which the process was completed. Using these criteria, we determined that 107 of the 117 exonerations that occurred before the end of 2004 were under threat of execution, and 10 exonerations were not under that threat. The significance of this classification is apparent. Of defendants sentenced to death since 1973, 35.8% had been resentenced to a prison term by the end of 2004. However, only 8.5% of capital exonerations (10 of 117) came from this group even though these prisoners were, by definition, at a later stage of their imprisonment than those who remained on death row. (Except for those who are exonerated—and a very small group who are resentenced to lesser penalties and eventually released—all prisoners who are sentenced to death do ultimately die in prison. They all start out on death row, some stay there until death by execution by other means, and the rest eventually are moved to the general prison population where they remain until they die.)

Our estimate of the rate of false convictions among death-sentenced defendants is based on the hypothesis that death-sentenced prisoners who remain under threat of execution are far more likely to be exonerated than those who remain in prison but no longer face that threat. We use a Cox proportional hazards model with a time-dependent covariate to test that hypothesis. We find, consistent with expectations, that death-sentenced defendants who are no longer under threat of execution had a rate of exoneration approximately one eighth of that for defendants who remained on death row, 0.131 ($P < 0.0001$) (with 95% confidence interval of 0.064–0.266).

Analysis

Our task is to estimate the cumulative probability over time of the event of interest, exoneration, in the population of death-sentenced defendants who remain under threat of execution. The temporal measure (t) is time from conviction. Estimating this probability is complicated by the structure of the population for two reasons. (*i*) Individual defendants joined this population across a 32-y period. Their duration in the study period varied from 1 to 32 y. (*ii*) All death-sentenced defendants began, at conviction, under threat of execution, but for most that threat, and their membership in the population of interest, ended within several years, usually because they were resentenced to life imprisonment. The net effect is that the number of defendants under threat of execution is a decreasing function of time from conviction, ranging from $n = 7,482$ at $t = 0$ y to $n = 0$ at $t = 30.7$ y.

To estimate this cumulative probability, we use survival analysis. This technique has been used in a related context, to estimate the rate of all reversals of death sentences in the United States. It is most commonly used, however, to evaluate the efficacy of medical treatments when not all patients experience the outcome of interest. The issue we address is analogous, but the analogy is counterintuitive.

We use survival analysis to assess the prospects of members of a population that is subject to a special risk. In the usual medical context, the condition that defines the population is a pathology such as Lyme disease or diabetes; for our study the defining condition is "death sentence." As a result of this condition, every member of this population is subject to the risk of a terminal event that might remove him from the group that has survived with this condition. In biomedical survival studies, that terminal event that is studied is death from the pathology in question; for our study it is exoneration. This is a counterintuitive equivalence: For our purposes, remaining in prison following a death sentence counts as "survival;" and exoneration, which removes the subject from prison, is analogous to "death" in the common context in which survival analysis is used.

Survival analysis is often used to evaluate the efficacy of a medical treatment that may reduce mortality from a pathology. In this study the "treatment" that lowers the probability of the terminal event of interest (exoneration) is removal of the threat of execution. (This too is a counterintuitive analogy. Exonerating an innocent defendant is, of course, a good thing for that defendant, but removal from death row is equivalent to a treatment that reduces the "risk" of exoneration.) Our focus, however, is not on the treated group (those removed from death row) but on those who remain untreated (defendants who remain under threat of execution and therefore at high risk of exoneration).

In this study, as in medical research, subjects may be removed from the population of interest by means other than the terminal event at issue. In survival analysis of a disease, the usual means of exit by other means are death from a different cause or discontinuation of participation in the study. In our study, all deaths after capital sentencing (by execution, suicide, or natural causes) remove the person from the population that is subject to the risk of execution. However, most removals from the population by means other than exoneration are by legal action that reduces the defendant's sentence to life in prison and thereby eliminates the threat of execution.

A primary difficulty in estimating the cumulative probability of exoneration is that some defendants were censored, i.e., they did not have an opportunity to be exonerated under threat of execution during the study period. Some defendants were removed from that threat during the study period but would have been exonerated had they remained under threat; others, who were sentenced to death relatively recently, remained under threat and had not been exonerated at the end of the study period but would have been exonerated at some later point if the study period were extended. As a result, a simple proportion of exonerated defendants to all defendants is a biased estimate of the cumulative probability of exoneration.

We therefore use the Kaplan–Meier estimator to calculate the cumulative probability of exoneration under threat of execution for death-sentenced defendants, by time from conviction through 2004. This estimator takes account of the censoring of observations caused by recency of incarceration on death row, death from suicide or natural causes, or other removals from the threat of execution. The Kaplan–Meier survival function estimates the probability of being event-free (remaining on death row) up to a given length of time from conviction. Its complement (1 minus the estimator) estimates the cumulative incidence of the event (exoneration) up to the given length of time from conviction. Unlike a simple proportion, the Kaplan–Meier estimator is unbiased in the presence of independent censoring (see further discussions in *Sensitivity Analysis*), and is completely nonparametric; it can be viewed as a censored data analog of the empirical distribution function.

As the data shows, the cumulative probability of exoneration for death-sentenced defendants who remained under threat of execution for 21.4 y was 4.1% (with a 95% confidence interval of 2.8–5.2%). [We replicated the Kaplan–Meier estimate of the cumulative probability of exoneration under threat of execution using the Fleming–Harrington estimator. Both results are virtually indistinguishable.]

This 4.1% estimate may approach the underlying rate of false convictions because it reflects the cumulative effect of a process that is uniquely efficient at detecting such errors. To rely on this estimate, however, two additional steps are necessary.

Sensitivity Analysis

An important assumption for the validity of the Kaplan–Meier estimator is that censoring events that remove subjects from consideration are statistically independent of the time to the event of interest if the subjects had not been removed. In this context, that assumption is plausible with respect to censoring by recency of conviction and by death from suicide or natural causes while under threat of execution. On the other hand, there are strong reasons to believe that both execution and removal from death row by legal procedures without exoneration are not independent of time-to-exoneration. Because the assumption of independence may be violated, sensitivity analysis is necessary.

Specifically, (*i*) 13% of death-sentenced inmates were removed from death row by execution (943 of 7,482). Some executed defendants may have been innocent, and, although none has been exonerated after execution, they might have been exonerated if they had remained alive and on death row. However, we expect that the proportion of innocent defendants is lower among those who are executed than among those who remain on death row. The threat of execution is the engine that drives the process of exonerating innocent death row prisoners, and it is likely that this process becomes more painstaking as inmates approach their execution dates. This concern about executing innocent defendants also drives a second bias: (*ii*) It increases the proportion of innocent defendants among the 36% of death row inmates who were removed from death row and resentenced to prison but not exonerated (2,675 or 7,482). Courts and executive officials explicitly recognize that it is appropriate to take the possibility of innocence into account in deciding whether to reverse a conviction for procedural error or commute a death sentence to life imprisonment, and a wealth of anecdotal evidence suggests that this practice is widespread. As a result, those who are resentenced to punishments less than death are more likely to be innocent than those who remain on death row.

In short, we believe that (*i*) executed defendants are less likely to have been exonerated if they had remained on death row than those who in fact remained on death row, and (*ii*) defendants who were removed from death row but remained in prison are more likely to have been exonerated if they had remained under threat of execution.

These two biases are not equivalent in magnitude. Nearly three times as many unexonerated death-sentenced defendants were resentenced to prison (2,675) as were executed (943). Even a modest increase in the proportion of innocent defendants among death-sentenced prisoners resentenced to life imprisonment, compared with those who remain on death row, would more than offset a complete absence of innocent defendants among those who are executed.

We use competing risks methodology, along with explicit assumptions about the counterfactual probability of exoneration for those who were executed or resentenced to prison, to develop a sensitivity analysis for the Kaplan–Meier estimate of the cumulative exoneration rate. First, we estimate the cumulative incidence of exoneration subject to the competing risks of execution and resentencing by 21.4 y after conviction, on the assumption that censoring by recency, suicide, or natural death was independent of these three event processes. The estimates of the probabilities of removal from risk of exoneration by exoneration under threat of execution, by execution itself, or by resentencing, are 2.2% (1.7%, 2.7%), 23.8% (22.3%, 25.3%), and 48.3% (46.7%, 50.0%), respectively. Thus, a defendant sentenced to death had an estimated 2.2% chance of being exonerated while under threat of execution by 21.4 y after conviction, assuming those executed or resentenced had zero chance of being exonerated (i.e., allowing for the competing risks of execution and resentencing).

Consider instead the assumption that, had they remained on death row, (*i*) those who were executed would have had zero chance of exoneration, and (*ii*) those who were resentenced would have had twice the chance of exoneration as the entire population of defendants sentenced to death. This yields the following estimate of the cumulative probability of exoneration, had those who were exonerated or resentenced instead remained on death row: 2.2% + 0 (23.8%) + 2 (2.2%) (48.3%) = 4.4%. Using the Delta method, the confidence interval for this estimate is 3.41–5.28%, assuming that the cumulative incidences of exoneration and resentencing have zero covariance.

A zero probability of exoneration for executed defendants had they remained on death row is necessarily, for the purposes of this estimate, a conservative assumption. We believe that the assumed probability of exoneration for those who were removed from death row and resentenced to prison, twice the mean for the population, is reasonable. We conclude that the Kaplan–Meier estimate we obtained is conservative. Indeed the same result we would obtain if we assume that the probability of exoneration for those resentenced to prison, had they remained on death row, is equal to or greater than 1.77 times the population average [2.2% + 0 (23.8%) + 1.77 (2.2%) (48.3%) = 4.1%].

Estimating False Convictions from Exonerations

Because there is no general method to accurately determine innocence in a criminal case, we use a proxy, exoneration: an official determination that a convicted defendant is no longer legally culpable for the crime for which he was condemned. There will be misclassifications. Some exonerated defendants are guilty of the crimes for which they were sentenced to death. We expect that such errors are rare, given the high barriers the American legal system imposes on convicted defendants in persuading authorities to reconsider their guilt. To date, one such case has come to light, and has been reclassified. Monte Carlo simulations reveal that the effect of such misclassifications on the cumulative rate of exoneration is linear: If 10% of exonerated defendants were in fact guilty, the mean cumulative rate of innocence for death-sentenced defendants would be 3.7% rather than 4.1% (95% confidence interval of 3.3–4.0%); if 20% were guilty, the mean rate would be 3.3% (95% confidence interval of 2.8–3.7%)

On the other side, some innocent defendants who remained on death row for more than 21.4 y but were not exonerated are misclassified as guilty. Some may still be exonerated; some may be executed; and most will likely die in prison, on death row or off, of natural causes or suicide. In the absence of better data we assume that the probability of a legal campaign to exonerate any prisoner under threat of death who has a plausible innocence claim is 1, and we assume that the probability of success for an innocent prisoner who remains under such threat for at least 21.4 y is also 1. These are necessarily conservative assumptions. To the extent that these probabilities are in fact less than 1, our estimate will understate the actual rate of false convictions.

The distribution of possible misclassifications is asymmetrical: 216 defendants remained on death row longer than 21.4 y, whereas only 107 were exonerated under threat of execution. Unless the process of death row exoneration is assumed to be unrealistically thorough, it is likely that the number of innocent death-sentenced defendants misclassified as guilty exceeds the number of guilty defendants exonerated under threat of execution and misclassified as innocent. [The proxy we use (the exoneration rate) is also important in its own right: It is a direct measure of the rate of death sentencing of defendants later determined to be legally not guilty.]

Taken together, the sensitivity analysis and the likely net effects of misclassification both point in the same direction and suggest that our 4.1% estimate of the rate of false conviction among death-sentenced defendants is conservative.

Discussion

We present a conservative estimate of the proportion of erroneous convictions of defendants sentenced to death in the United States from 1973 through 2004, 4.1%. This is a unique finding; there are no other reliable estimates of the rate of false conviction in any context. The main source of potential bias is the accuracy of our classification of cases as true or false convictions. On that issue it is likely that we have an undercount, that there are more innocent death row defendants who have not been identified and exonerated than guilty ones who have been exonerated in error.

The most charged question in this area is different: How many innocent defendants have been put to death? We cannot estimate that number directly but we believe it is comparatively low. If the rate were the same as our estimate for false death sentences, the number of innocents executed in the United States in the past 35 y would be more than 50. We do not believe that has happened. Our data and the experience of practitioners in the field both indicate that the criminal justice system goes to far greater lengths to avoid executing innocent defendants than to prevent them from remaining in prison indefinitely. One way to do so is to disproportionately reverse death sentences in capital cases in which the accuracy of the defendants' convictions is in doubt and to resentence them to life imprisonment, a practice that makes our estimate of the rate of error conservative. However, no process of removing potentially innocent defendants from the execution queue can be foolproof. With an error rate at trial over 4%, it is all but certain that several of the 1,320 defendants executed since 1977 were innocent.

It is possible that the death-sentencing rate of innocent defendants has changed over time. No specific evidence points in that direction, but the number and the distribution of death sentences have changed dramatically in the past 15 y. One change, however, is unlikely to have much impact: the advent of DNA identification technology. DNA evidence is useful primarily in rape rather than homicide investigations. Only 13% of death row exonerations since 1973 (18 of 142) resulted from postconviction DNA testing, so the availability of preconviction testing will have at most a modest effect on that rate.

Unfortunately, we cannot generalize from our findings on death sentences to the rate of false convictions in any broader category of crime. Capital prosecutions, and to a lesser extent murder cases in general, are handled very differently from other criminal cases. There are theoretical reasons to believe that the rate of false conviction may be higher for murders in general, and for capital murders in particular, than for other felony convictions, primarily because the authorities are more likely to pursue difficult cases with weak evidence of guilt if one or more people have been killed. However, there are no data that confirm or refute this hypothesis.

We do know that the rate of error among death sentences is far greater than Justice Scalia's reassuring 0.027%. That much is apparent directly from the number of death row exonerations that have already occurred. Our research adds the disturbing news that most innocent defendants who have been sentenced to death have not been exonerated, and many—including the great majority of those who have been resentenced to life in prison—probably never will be.

This is only part of a disturbing picture. Fewer than half of all defendants who are convicted of capital murder are ever sentenced to death in the first place (e.g., 49.1% in Missouri, 29% in Philadelphia, and 31% in New Jersey). Sentencing juries, like other participants in the process, worry about the execution of innocent defendants. Interviews with jurors who participated in capital sentencing proceedings indicate that lingering doubts about the defendant's guilt is the strongest available predictor of a sentence of life imprisonment rather than death. It follows that the rate of innocence must be higher for convicted capital defendants who are not sentenced to death than for those who are. The net result is that the great majority of innocent defendants who are convicted of capital murder in the United States are neither executed nor exonerated. They are sentenced, or resentenced to prison for life, and then forgotten.

10

Crime Victims Also Suffer from Wrongful Convictions

Seri Irazola, Erin Williamson, Julie Stricker, and Emily Niedzwiecki

Seri Irazola is a director of the Office of Research and Evaluation at the National Institute of Justice. Erin Williamson serves as a survivor support coordinator and project manager for Love146. Julie Stricker works with the International Justice Mission. Emily Niedzwiecki is assoicated with ICF.

Much has been done to help people wrongfully convicted of a crime, especially in terms of offering resources that can be used to garner exoneration. But for a long time, the effects of exoneration on the victims of crimes have been largely put to the side. Recent research shows that victims suffer greatly when wrongfully convicted individuals are exonerated and released. Studies outline a wide range of emotions that victims suffer, with a particular focus on fear. Victims often fear that wrongfully convicted individuals will seek revenge and cause them harm. Various justice system professionals suggest ways to help victims overcome their traumas.

We need to better understand how wrongful convictions affect the original crime victims and improve systemic support available to them.

"Addressing the Impact of Wrongful Convictions on Crime Victims," by Seri Irazola, Erin Williamson, Julie Stricker and Emily Niedzwiecki, National Institute of Justice, December 2014.

When a wrongfully convicted individual is exonerated, the original crime victim may experience feelings of guilt, fear, helplessness, devastation and depression. For some victims, the impact of the wrongful conviction may be comparable to—or even worse than—that of their original victimization.

These are the findings of an NIJ-funded study examining how wrongful convictions affect the original crime victims, an area in which no prior empirical research had been conducted. Researchers from ICF International conducted in-depth studies to identify the shared experiences and service needs of the original crime victims in 11 cases of wrongful conviction. Recognizing the sensitive nature of the study, the researchers initially contacted victims through third parties, such as district attorney's offices and innocence commissions that had pre-existing relationships with the victims. They also used what is called "snowball sampling," meaning they worked with participating victims and stakeholders to reach out to crime victims in other cases of wrongful conviction and to identify service providers, law enforcement officers, prosecutors, attorneys and family members who supported victims during the exonerations. In total, researchers interviewed 33 individuals:

- Eleven victims (including immediate family members in cases of homicide)
- Nine prosecutors
- Four service providers
- Three law enforcement officers
- Two family members
- Two individuals who provided victims with legal advice
- Two innocence commission members

The study found that wrongful convictions have a significant impact on the original crime victims and exposed a lack of services available to them. The researchers also noted that although we have made significant strides over the past three decades to identify wrongfully convicted individuals and to help them gain their freedom and transition to life after exoneration, additional research is still needed to fully understand the experiences and address the needs of the original crime victims during this process. As one victim told researchers, "For [several] years, I had been quite comfortable with my role as the victim. When the exoneration happened, that exoneree became the victim, and I, the rape victim, became the offender. The roles switch, and it's a role you don't know what to do with."

A Closer Look at the Cases*

The 11 case studies involved nonfederal violent crimes committed in six states; eight of the crimes took place in urban communities. Many of the cases involved multiple crimes. In order of frequency, the offenses were:

- Rape
- Homicide
- Sexual assault
- Burglary
- Attempted homicide
- Breaking and entering
- Other sexual offenses

Twelve individuals were wrongfully convicted for these crimes. Eyewitness misidentification, invalidated or improper forensic evidence and analysis, false testimony by informants, false confessions, and ineffective legal counsel contributed to the wrongful convictions.

In five cases, law enforcement officers, victim advocates or other officials notified the victim of the potential wrongful conviction during the reinvestigation—for example, when a DNA test had been ordered or when the case had been opened for a formal review in response to an innocence commission. In one case, an official notified the victim after the wrongfully convicted individual had already been exonerated. In four cases, victims learned of the potential wrongful conviction through third parties, such as reporters or legal representatives for the wrongfully convicted individuals. And in one case, notification was not necessary because the victim believed in the wrongfully convicted person's innocence from the time of the original trial and was actively involved in the appeal and exoneration process.

In nine of the 11 cases, law enforcement identified the actual offender through a confession, DNA testing or new evidence. Three of these offenders were prosecuted and convicted. In three cases, the statute of limitations had passed. In the remaining cases, the offenders were not prosecuted for reasons specific to the individual cases; however, in a few of these cases, the actual offenders were incarcerated for other offenses.

How Wrongful Convictions May Affect Victims

More than half of the victims in the study described the impact of the wrongful conviction as being comparable to—or worse than—that of their original victimization. Many said they were in shock when they first heard about the exoneration. The majority of the victims also reported intense feelings of guilt. This was especially true for the two-thirds of victims in the study who provided eyewitness identification. One victim recounted, "It was harder going through the revictimization than it was through the rape. ... Now you have the same feelings of that pain. You have the same scariness. You have the same fear. You have the same panic, but now you have this flood of guilt on top of it."

As with many cases of wrongful conviction, most of the cases studied received media attention, generating notoriety for both the wrongfully convicted individuals and the crime victims. As one law enforcement officer explained, "You see exoneration cases. You see the media's flash when [the wrongfully convicted individual is] walking out of the courthouse. Everybody is excited, and yet quietly sitting at home by themselves are the victims." Some of the victims felt that the media insinuated that they had intentionally misidentified the wrongfully convicted individuals. Many found the anger directed toward them in blogs and comments that followed news articles particularly painful. One victim stated, "This is the thing—your name's not out there, but you are out there. This is your case. This is something that happened to your body. This is what happened to your mind, to your life. ... I didn't give anybody permission to put this out in the newspaper."

The crime victims reported being afraid of the wrongfully convicted individual following the exoneration. One victim said, "My initial thought was [the wrongfully convicted individual] is going to kill me. [They] will hurt me, and if [they] can't get to me, [they] will get to my children. So I was hyperalert. The children could not leave my side. I went to school and told the teachers, 'They are to stay with you every second.' That went on for almost two years." The crime victims also reported being afraid of the actual offenders. Some experienced helplessness, devastation and depression; at least one felt suicidal.

Improving Support for Victims

When asked for recommendations, victims and stakeholders spoke of the need to improve notification, information and services for the original crime victims in cases of wrongful conviction. In all of the case studies, those interviewed agreed that the criminal justice system should provide initial notification. Victims and other stakeholders recommended that, when appropriate and possible, officials involved in the original case should notify the crime victim. When this is not possible, many stakeholders suggested having a victim service provider present. Others stressed that law enforcement or prosecutors should be present, especially in cases that may involve additional litigation.

Interviewees generally advised that officials should notify the original crime victim in person. One service provider suggested that officials dress in plain clothes to avert unwanted attention or speculation from community members. Service providers noted that when in-person notification is not possible, telephone notification is preferable to a letter or other form of communication.

Recommendations varied regarding the timing of the initial notification. Law enforcement and prosecutors were reluctant to disrupt victims' lives every time there was a claim of innocence, whereas the crime victims expressed a desire to be notified early in the process. This study did identify a complicating factor: the varying amount of time it takes for a wrongful conviction to be confirmed and then for the wrongfully convicted individual to be released. Victims and stakeholders agreed that the original crime victims should not be blindsided by the exoneration or find out after the wrongfully convicted individual has been released.

Victims and stakeholders stressed that the crime victims are often unfamiliar with the criminal justice system and need information explaining the exoneration process. Service providers noted that victims want to understand the process and how it may affect their lives, well-being and safety. Victims who received regular updates emphasized the importance of these updates, saying that the updates made them feel that they were part of the process. However, it cannot be assumed that all victims will want ongoing updates. Victims and stakeholders recommended asking the crime victims during the initial notification what types of information and case updates they want to receive and how they want to receive them.

Several victims in the study who provided eyewitness identification said that learning how misidentifications may occur helped them process their reactions and understand the wrongful conviction. Some officials, however, pointed out that providing such information might not be appropriate or legally advisable for law enforcement. Victims also said that information on how memories are formed helped them understand why they continued to envision the wrongfully convicted individual when they thought about the crime.

Recognizing that victims are often unable to absorb the information they are given, especially during initial notification, stakeholders recommended giving crime victims printed materials to refer to when they have questions. In addition, stakeholders suggested giving victims a point of contact within the criminal justice system, whom they can reach with additional questions or concerns.

Victims said that notification and information should be provided in a neutral manner. Key stakeholders reported that crime victims usually take a strong position for or against the exoneration, but trying to convince them to take one position or the other is not always helpful. In addition, victims who had been assured that DNA tests postconviction would confirm the convicted person's guilt reported that the exoneration was especially difficult because they had never considered that a wrongful conviction was even a possibility.

Both victims and service providers recommended safety planning for crime victims. Only one victim interviewed for this study received safety planning, and that was after they specifically requested it. In general, victims remembered being told not to worry about safety. When discussing the importance of safety planning, one service provider explained that regardless of whether there is an actual threat, crime victims who perceive danger genuinely fear for their safety and the safety of their families.

Interviewees also highlighted the importance of counseling services in helping crime victims come to terms with the wrongful conviction. Given the unique nature of these cases, interviewees recommended that counseling services be provided by someone with formal training and experience working with victims of trauma. They also suggested making peer support available. Several victims recommended establishing a national network, operated by a neutral victim-centered organization, to facilitate peer support across jurisdictions. All of the victims interviewed for this study who received peer support were direct victims of a crime; additional research is needed to explore the benefits of peer support for other victims, such as family members in cases of homicide.

Finally, attorneys interviewed for this study recommended that all victims in wrongful conviction cases receive access to independent legal counsel. One attorney suggested that counsel have expertise in criminal defense, as well as training and experience working with victims of trauma. More research is needed to examine the legal considerations for victims in cases of wrongful conviction.

* This article uses gender-neutral language (*they, them, their, themselves*) and omits demographic and other identifying information to protect the identities of the victims who participated in the study.

11

Life After Exoneration

Saskia de Melker

Saskia de Melker is a Peabody Award–winning broadcast producer. She reports and writes feature stories for PBS NewsHour Weekend and New England Public Radio.

Four different men share their stories of how they are getting along after being exonerated. Each story is different, but taken as a whole one can begin to understand the difficulties that wrongfully convicted people must face when they are released from prison. A big challenge is figuring out how to support themselves. Another is the fear they feel of being re-imprisoned. A common theme is that these individuals would give anything to get back the years they lost in prison.

When a wrongfully convicted person gets released from prison, it is a major news event: Local television crews capture the first moments of freedom and the speeches on the steps of the state capital, audiences empathize as they grapple with gratitude and rage, and the exonerees take their first steps into an uncertain future.

Jeffrey Deskovic, who was in prison for 16 years after being wrongfully convicted for the rape and murder of his high school classmate, said it was the most surreal moment of his life: "It felt like a dream," he said. "When I stepped up to the microphones at the press conference, I asked 'Is this really happening?'"

"Four Wrongfully Convicted Men, Four Very Different Outcomes," by Saskia de Melker, NewsHour Productions LLC, November 9, 2014. Reprinted by permission.

But when the limelight fades, the wrongfully convicted face the reality of navigating the world they were yanked from, often with limited financial and social support.

According to the Innocence Project, it takes exonerees three years on average to receive any compensation after their release. More than a quarter get nothing. Among those who are paid, 81 percent get less than $50,000 for each year of wrongful imprisonment.

NewsHour spoke to a number of exonerated men from different states about their experiences reintegrating post-release. All of them, regardless of compensation, say they would pay anything to have the years they lost in prison back.

Jeffrey Deskovic, New York

Age: 41
Exonerated: 2006
Years in Prison: 16 years
Compensation: Over $13,000,000 (so far)

At age 16, Deskovic was wrongfully convicted of the rape and murder of his high school classmate. After nearly two decades behind bars, a DNA test finally exonerated him.

Those first five years were very difficult, he said. Released at age 33, he had never lived alone or even gotten a driver's license. "It was overwhelming. I felt like I didn't belong, like a fish out of water."

Deskovic filed federal civil rights lawsuits against the various municipalities and officials involved in his conviction. After an arduous and lengthy legal process, he was awarded more than $13 million in 2011. Just last month he won a separate $41 million dollar judgement.

"I would be willing to not only give the money back, I'd be willing to go into debt for that amount of money, maybe even double it, to have had my years back and had a normal life," said Deskovic.

Deskovic used part of his settlement money to set up his own foundation to help investigate other possible wrongful convictions across the country as well as offer financial and social support to other exonerees.

"I'm trying to make my suffering count for something," said Deskovic.

Johnny Pinchback, Texas

Age: 59
Exonerated: 2011
Years in Prison: 27 years
Compensation: $2,133,333

Pinchback was convicted for the rape of two teenage girls, who misidentified him in a police lineup. It wasn't until another exonerated man (who had been in prison with Pinchback) helped him appeal for a DNA test that the evidence proved he was not the perpetrator.

Within months of being released he received a lump sum payment of approximately $80,000 for each year he was in prison from the state of Texas, and he'll also continue to receive monthly annuity payments.

"It could never pay for the time I did [in prison] , but at least now I can have some peace." he said.

He said he is now enjoying a normal life. He bought a ranch outside of Dallas where he spends time with his wife, his mom, and his dogs. Pinchback served six years in the military prior to his conviction and prison time.

"After so many years of being told exactly what to do and where to be, I'm enjoying doing what I want to do."

Pinchback is just one of dozens of exonerees from Dallas County, which boasts more wrongfully convicted men than any other region in the country. He offers support and advice to other exonerees when they are let out.

"I warn them that everyone will be asking you for part of your [compensation] money once those checks start rolling in, whether they supported you during your prison time or not," said

Pinchback. The advice he gives them: "Take care of the people you love, but don't let anyone take advantage of you."

Drew Whitley, Pennsylvania

Age: 58
Exonerated: 2006
Years in Prison: 18 years
Compensation: $0

In 1989, Whitley was convicted for the murder of a young woman in Dusquene, Pennsylvania. He spent 18 years behind bars before DNA confirmed that hairs found in the ski mask of the killer did not belong to him, and he was set free.

He returned to his hometown of Braddock, Penn., where he spends most afternoons cleaning up the local meat shop in exchange for food. He gets by on a social security check of about $700 a month. Just over a year ago he moved out of his mother's home into an apartment that costs nearly half his monthly check.

Without a compensation package in Pennsylvania, Drew Whitley sued in federal court. Even though a judge agreed that police officers were negligent in their investigation of his case, she ruled against Whitley stating that he did not prove intentional misconduct. He lost his appeals of the decision.

In addition to his financial struggles, Whitley is still wrestling with the demons of his past. "Every time somebody walks up the hallway steps, I look out the peephole, because I think they might be coming to get me," he said. "I wake up with nightmares that I'm still locked up."

Alan Newton, New York

Age: 53
Exonerated: 2006
Years in Prison: 22 years
Compensation: $0

Newton served 22 years in prison for the rape, robbery and assault of a young woman who misidentified him. He spent years appealing for a DNA test, which the police claimed to have lost. It was finally found and tested proving that Newton was not guilty.

He says people now know that he didn't do the crime but they have a different concern about him as an exoneree.

"They wonder if I picked up bad habits and became criminalized while I was in prison for all those years," he said. "I feel like I have to defend myself against that fear."

In 2010, he won a federal lawsuit and was awarded $18.5 million by a jury. But Newton hasn't seen a dime of that money: a judge reversed the jury's verdict stating that Newton didn't sufficiently prove intentional misconduct in his case, only negligence. Newton appealed but four years later, he's still awaiting a decision from an appellate court. "It's very frustrating, but I've learned patience with the legal system" he said.

Even without any compensation, Newton has made the most of his exonerated life. He got his Bachelor's degree in business administration and now works for the City University of New York as a research associate. He speaks frequently about law enforcement practices leading to wrongful convictions and plans to apply for law school.

Still, he feels he can't truly move on.

"At this point, it's not even about blaming someone. I just want closure and to be able to move on with life. That's what the money is about as much as anything else," he said.

12

The Media Controls How the Public Views Crime

Alice Courtauld

Alice Courtauld is a law student at King's College in London.

Media consumers are bombarded by crime-related stories in the news on a daily basis. Is the audience getting a distorted view of the facts as a result? Studies suggest this is the case. Media companies and the journalists reporting for them have an agenda: to grasp and hold onto audiences. To do this, the media uses a variety of strategies. To cover the 24/7 news cycle, the media overreports crime incidents and keeps the stories in the public eye. Studies show that as a result of this pattern, people are becoming increasingly afraid of crime and have an irrational feeling that crime is worse than it actually is.

The mass media and individuals have an obsession with crime; libraries and bookstores are full of crime fiction and non fiction books, and newspaper devote roughly 30 per cent of their coverage to crime. However some groups argue that this is dangerous in that it presents a distorted view of crime; both in the selection of crime news stories, depending on their newsworthiness, and the over-representation and exaggeration of certain crimes, which can increase the risk of some individuals believing that they are more likely to be a victim.

"How the Media Controls Our Perceptions of Crime," by Alice Courtauld, Shout Out UK, November 8, 2014. Reprinted by permission.

The media plays a key role in agenda setting in relation to crime and deviance. Agenda setting refers to the media's influence over the issues that people think about. The mass media clearly can't report every single criminal or deviant act that occurs, and media personnel are necessarily very selective in the incidents that they choose either to report or ignore. Naturally people are only able to discuss and form opinions about the crime and deviance that they have been informed about, provided by the agenda setting media. This results in people's perceptions of crime and deviance in society being influenced by what media personnel choose to include or leave out of their newspapers, television programmes, films or websites. Media representation overwhelmingly therefore influences what people believe about crime regardless of whether these impressions are true or not.

Reiner (2007) points out that media coverage of crime and deviance is filtered through journalists' sense of what makes an event newsworthy—a good story that media audiences want to know about. The idea of this is driven by what are known as "news values." These are values and assumptions held by editors and journalists which guide them in choosing what is newsworthy, and therefore what to report on and what to leave out, and how to present these stories. This notion means that journalists tend to include and play up those elements of a story that make it more newsworthy, and the stories that are most likely to be reported are those with dramatic aspects.

In relation to crime specifically, Jewkes (2004) suggest these news events have to be considered significant or dramatic enough to be in the news—a single rape may make the local newspaper, but a serial rapist might become a national story, for example, the Yorkshire ripper. Crime becomes newsworthy when it can be presented as serious, random and unpredictable enough so that a moral panic occurs in the sense that we all get scared of becoming a victim ourselves. For example, the 'war on terror' meant that initially many people felt that every person in the UK was at a risk. Events, namely violent ones, accompanied by film, CCTV or mobile phone footage are more newsworthy as they enable the media to provide a visual and dramatic impact for the audiences.

The August 2011 riots demonstrate this. This new media enabled almost instant pictures to be obtained directly from the riots. Crime and deviance, even if quite trivial involving celebrities or more powerful people whether they are victims or offenders, is seen as more newsworthy than that involving ordinary people. The MPs' expenses scandal is one example; though many businesses make additional claims on their expenses, this however rarely hits the news. Finally, children as offenders or victims of crime have the potential to be newsworthy. Sex crimes, women as victims and non-criminal sexual deviance like bondage, domination and sadomasochism, are generally more newsworthy.

As these newsworthy stories appear on TV and explicitly in the tabloids, research evidence shows that there is a link between media use and fear of crime. In the USA Gerbner found that heavy users of TV (over 4 hours a day) had higher levels of fear of crime. They found a correlation between media consumption and fear of crime, especially physical attacks or muggings. If reader or viewers are constantly bombarded with certain images then this could lead to a form of moral panic. After 9/11 a minority of white British felt all Muslims were a threat to their safety.

Furthermore Greer (2005) found that all media tends to exaggerate the extent of violent crime. The tabloid 'red top' newspapers are always seeking out newsworthy stories of crime and deviance, in order to exploit the possibilities for a good story by dramatising, exaggerating, over-reporting and sensationalising certain crimes out of proportion just to generate audience interest and attract readers.

Despite the fact that most crime is fairly routine, trivial and non-dramatic, TV programmes such as *Crimewatch* often pick up on the more serious and violent offences like sexual assault, murder or armed robbery—with reconstructions giving quite a frightening insight into the crime. This focus on the dramatic side of crime is a routine feature on TV programmes or film as well as news reports, and gives a false and misleading impression of the real extent of such crimes.

Reiner points out that crime fiction presents property crime less frequently than is shown in crime statistics but the property crime it does portray is far more serious than most recorded offences. He concludes that the picture of crime shown by the media is the opposite of that shown by statistics on crime. Such media representations tend to create distorted perceptions of crime among the majority of the public, exaggerate its threat and unnecessarily increase the public's fear of crime.

Even if much of what is reported is untrue or exaggerated it may be enough to whip up a moral panic. The media can cause crime and deviance through labelling. Moral entrepreneurs may use the media to put pressure on the authorities to do something about the problem. This can lead to negative labelling of the behaviour and a change in law. Thereby acts that were once legal become illegal. Part of this is the creation of moral panic – an exaggerated overreaction by society to a perceived problem, usually driven by the media where the reaction enlarges the problem out of all proportion to its real seriousness.

Stan Cohen's work, *Folk Devils and Moral Panics*, illustrates this. His initial work focused on the minor confrontation in Clacton, 1964. The media overreacted in three seminal ways. Firstly, the media exaggerated the numbers involved and the extent of the violence via headlines like "day of terror by scooter gangs." Secondly, the media regularly assumed and predicted that further violence would result. And finally, the media used symbolism; the hairstyles, clothes, bikes and scooters, the music of Mods and Rockers, were all labelled and associated with violence. The media portrayal of events produced a deviance amplification spiral by making it seem that the problem was spreading. This leads to calls for greater activity by the police and courts, and further labelling and marginalisation of Mods and Rockers. The media further amplified the deviance by defining the subculture, therefore many youths joined these groups and were involved in future clashes in what became a self-fulfilling prophecy of escalating conflict, due to polarisation. Individuals reading and seeing these reports felt that they were at risk from all young people who dressed as Mods or Rockers.

However McRobbie and Thornton say moral panics are so frequent that they have little impact on the audience. They suggest that the concept of moral panic as used by Cohen in the case of the Mods and Rockers is now outdated and no longer a useful concept in the contemporary world. This is because new media technology, the growing sophistication of media audiences in a media-saturated society, and intense competition both between different types of media and media companies, have changed the reporting of and reaction to events that might once have caused a moral panic. There is now a diverse range of media reports and interpretations of events and of opinions and reactions to these events by the public. People are now much more sceptical of media interpretations and less likely to believe them. This means that it has become more difficult for the media to define issues or evens in such a way that can develop into a moral panic. This is also made more difficult by the way that news reporting now involves 24/7 rolling news, which is constantly broadcast and instantly updated. As a consequence stories have a short shelf life and are unlikely to sustain an audience's interest and are unlikely to be newsworthy for long enough to generate a moral panic.

Its important to adopt and take note of both of these schools of thought, for when combined and synthesis is found, we become weary of the news. Of course it is helpful to be informed of headlines in the news. But one must realise that this does not reflect the true extent of crime. The 2012 statistics for example show that, overwhelmingly, the guilty criminal for crimes such as homicide related to women is the husband, rather than the violent stranger that may be lurking in the dark alleyways. We must therefore digest the news but also stay vigilant.

13

Exonerated Individuals May Not Recoup Fines, Fees, or Court Costs

Ian Millhiser

Ian Millhiser is the justice editor at the news site ThinkProgress. He is the author of Injustices: The Supreme Court's History of Comforting the Comfortable and Afflicting the Afflicted.

What could be worse than being wrongfully convicted of a crime? Perhaps paying the hefty court fees and fines associated with criminal charges and then not being reimbursed for the money after being found innocent. It sounds hard to believe, but that is exactly what often happens, which is especially clear when considering cases in Colorado. According to the states' Exoneration Act, a person can only recover previously paid-out fees and fines if they can prove undeniable innocence, which, according to experts, is extremely difficult.

I magine that you are hauled into court for a crime you did not commit, convicted, then forced to turn over a fortune in fines, fees and court costs as a result. Then, after an appeals court throws out your conviction and the charges against you are dropped, you are told that you aren't allowed to have your money back—even though the state's only basis for taking that money from you was an invalid trial judgment.

"Supreme Court Considers if Exonerated People Can Be Charged the Same Fines and Fees as the Guilty," by Ian Millhiser, ThinkProgress, Center for American Progress, January 9, 2017. Reprinted by permission.

In most states, this wouldn't happen. Yet, under the Colorado Supreme Court's 2015 decision in *People v. Nelson*, an exonerated defendant who seeks to recover money that was unlawfully taken from him due to an illegal conviction is out of luck. Though the facts of *Nelson* are somewhat less stark than the hypothetical scenario described above, its sweeping holding would potentially allow the state to collect thousands or even millions of dollars worth of fines and fees from someone convicted of a crime, and then refuse to give it back after that person is exonerated.

"Due process does not require a defendant to be compensated automatically for the time she spent incarcerated while seeking an appeal or new trial," Chief Justice Nancy Rice wrote for her court. "Similarly, due process does not require an automatic refund of fines paid in connection with a conviction during that time."

This decision—along with a similar, consolidated case—is now before the Supreme Court of the United States in *Nelson v. Colorado*.

Both cases involve individuals who were convicted of crimes and then later exonerated. Shannon Nelson was convicted of sexual assault based, in part, on the testimony of a witness who was not property qualified as an expert. After an appeals court threw out her conviction, Nelson was retried and acquitted. Similarly, Louis Alonzo Madden was convicted of sex crimes, but his convictions were thrown out and prosecutors decided not to retry the case.

Nelson and Madden were both hit by a complicated mix of fees, surcharges, and other costs intended to fund the court system, pay for various programs, and provide restitution to their alleged victims. By the time they were exonerated, Nelson had paid $702.10 of these charges and Madden had paid $1,977.75. Now, they want their money back.

According to their attorneys, getting that money back wouldn't be a problem if they lived in any other state. "Colorado appears to be the only state that does not refund this money when a conviction is reversed," according to Nelson and Madden's brief.

Just a few years ago, it is likely that Colorado law would have allowed the two exonerees to be reimbursed. In the Colorado Supreme Court's 1961 decision in *Toland v. Strohl*, the court ordered that "the parties be placed in *status quo* by refund to the defendant of the sums paid as fine and costs" after his conviction was reversed. In 2013, however, Colorado enacted its Exoneration Act. As Nelson and Madden's attorneys explain in their brief, this law was intended to provide extraordinary compensation (as much as $120,000 per year of incarceration) to certain rare individuals who are imprisoned and then not simply exonerated, but determined to be actually innocent. To obtain this relief, however, a person convicted of a crime must prove, by "clear and convincing evidence," that they are innocent.

Thus, the Exoneration Act does not apply to people who have their convictions thrown out because the state lacked sufficient evidence to convict them. Unlike in a criminal trial, where the state must prove a defendant's guilt beyond a reasonable doubt, the Exoneration Act only provides relief to people who can affirmatively prove their own innocence—and who can overcome a high burden of proof in the process.

It is very rare that a defendant can meet this very high burden, which essentially requires them to prove a negative. According to Nelson and Madden's brief, the state legislature "projected that compensation under the Act would be awarded to only one defendant every five years."

It is unlikely that the state legislature intended for this rarely invoked law to be the only source of relief available to exonerates hit by fines or fees. Nevertheless, in its *Nelson* opinion, the Colorado Supreme Court held that *Toland* no longer applies to people like Nelson and Madden. If they can't obtain relief under the Exoneration Act, they are out of luck.

This is an especially harsh result because of the relatively small amounts of money at stake in their cases. The $702.10 Nelson seeks and the $1,977.75 Madden seeks are hardly chump change, but they are far less than a lawyer would charge to bring a case on either exonerees' behalf. As Colorado Justice William Hood explained in a dissenting opinion, "defendants with meritorious claims paying hourly rates could find themselves throwing good money after bad, while the relatively low amounts available will likely prevent most defendants from retaining counsel on a contingency basis."

Perhaps because Colorado's refusal to reimburse people like Nelson and Madden is so unusual, there is no Supreme Court precedent that speaks directly to this problem—although several lower courts have sided with exonerees in similar circumstances. The closest analogy in the high Court's own precedents is tax cases establishing that "the Due Process Clause requires the State to afford taxpayers a meaningful opportunity to secure postpayment relief for taxes already paid pursuant to a tax scheme ultimately found unconstitutional."

There are marginal issues within *Nelson* that do present difficult legal questions. A portion of the money Nelson and Madden paid, for example, was used as restitution for their alleged victims. Under Colorado law, moreover, an order of restitution is considered a civil (not a criminal) order.

Defendants in civil cases do not enjoy the same very high "beyond a reasonable doubt" standard that protects criminal defendants, so it is possible for someone to be found not guilty of a criminal charge and then still held liable to their alleged victim in a civil proceeding—just ask O.J. Simpson. Perhaps Colorado could defend its practice of issuing a criminal sentence and a civil restitution order simultaneously in the same proceeding. Although, even in this circumstance, it's far from clear why the civil restitution order wasn't vacated by Nelson and Madden's exoneration.

But the Colorado Supreme Court's decision sweeps well past these marginal issues. If "due process does not require an automatic refund of fines paid in connection with a conviction" while their case was on appeal, then there could be many circumstances where a person is exonerated and receives very little, if any, relief from the court's order dissolving their conviction.

Imagine, for example, a criminal defendant who is ordered to pay a $10,000 fine in addition to a relatively brief prison sentence. Under the Colorado Supreme Court's rule, so long as the defendant pays this fine in full before their conviction is overruled on appeal, the state is under no constitutional obligation to give the money back.

Moreover, if this defendant had already served their full prison sentence before their successful appeal is decided, a court order exonerating them would leave them in virtually the same position they would have been in even if their conviction remained in place. They are already free from prison. They can't recover the money they lost unless they can clear the very high bar set by the Exoneration Act. At most, they can try to put their life back together with a newly cleared record.

Meanwhile, the state would receive a $10,000 windfall because it obtained an unlawful conviction that was later tossed out by an appeals court.

If the Supreme Court permits such a result, the consequences could be catastrophic for residents of communities like Ferguson, Missouri, where courts use snowballing fines and fees to fund local government, often immiserating low-income residents in the process.

Under the Colorado Supreme Court's rule in *Nelson*, a person hit with such fines and fees could be exonerated of the crime that allowed the state to take their money in the first place, and yet be left unable to recover the money that was unlawfully taken from them.

14

How Should States Compensate the Wrongfully Convicted?

Scott Rodd

Scott Rodd is a journalist focusing on law and policy issues. He has written for the Sacramento Business Journal *and the Pew Charitable Trusts.*

This viewpoint examines the ways in which various states address the issue of compensating wrongfully convicted individuals. While Congress passed a bill in 2004 to guarantee compensation for time wrongfully spent imprisoned, the reality of how individuals are compensated varies greatly from state to state. Many argue that recouping money lost to court fees and years out of the workforce is necessary for successful re-entry into society, but the specifics of how this should be enacted are up in the air.

In April 2000, 23-year-old Floyd Bledsoe sat in an Oskaloosa, Kansas, courtroom awaiting the verdict in his first-degree murder trial in the death of his 14-year-old sister-in-law, Zetta "Camille" Arfmann. Throughout the trial, he maintained his innocence. But the jury entered the courtroom and declared him guilty.

Bledsoe was sentenced to life in prison plus 16 years, but doubts about his involvement in the murder lingered. The crime scene yielded little physical evidence, and Bledsoe's brother, Tom, 25, had originally confessed to the murder before recanting and pinning the crime on Floyd.

After years of fruitless court challenges, Bledsoe was vindicated in a gut-wrenching twist: In 2015, Tom Bledsoe confessed to the murder in a suicide note before asphyxiating himself. Within a month, a judge vacated Bledsoe's conviction and he was released from prison. The day of his release, Bledsoe recalls, was a mixture of celebration and mourning.

"Before I was locked up, I had 40 acres, livestock, a wife and kids," he said. "When I was released, I had nothing … I lost my family, my job, my reputation—everything."

Bledsoe found little support as he adjusted to life outside of prison, including from the state that locked him up for more than 15 years. A bill before the Kansas Legislature would make up for part of that by making him eligible for $80,000 for each year he spent behind bars.

A steady increase in exonerations in recent years, often a result of new DNA-testing capability, has prompted lawmakers in states like Kansas to consider legislation that guarantees compensation for those who are wrongfully convicted and imprisoned. And in the 32 states that have compensation laws, some lawmakers have sought to increase the amount of compensation exonerated individuals would receive, expand the eligibility for compensation or streamline the process for getting it.

It's only just that states provide compensation to people who are wrongly convicted and imprisoned, advocates for the wrongly convicted say.

"When an innocent person is deprived of liberty because of a wrongful conviction, regardless of fault, the government has a responsibility to do all it can to foster that person's re-entry in order to help restore some sense of justice," said Maddy deLone, executive director of the Innocence Project, a nonprofit legal organization that specializes in wrongful conviction cases. "Fair compensation is part of that."

According to the National Registry of Exonerations, 2,000 wrongfully convicted individuals have been exonerated for state and federal crimes since 1989. In 2016, there were 166 exonerations nationwide—the most since the registry was established nearly 30 years ago.

In 2004, Congress passed the Justice for All Act with bipartisan support. The law guarantees individuals exonerated of federal crimes $50,000 for every year spent in prison and $100,000 for every year spent on death row.

From state to state, however, those who are exonerated are not guaranteed the same rights or compensation after a conviction is overturned. "It really matters where you're convicted," said Amol Sinha, state policy advocate at the Innocence Project.

In Texas, a state known for its tough-on-crime posture, the exonerated are paid $80,000 for every year spent in prison and are eligible for monthly annuity payments after release. The state's generous compensation law has added up over time. In the last 25 years, Texas has paid over $93 million to wrongfully convicted individuals.

Wisconsin, on the other hand, pays $5,000 for every year spent in prison, capped at a maximum of $25,000. Some states offer in-kind benefits in addition to monetary compensation. Vermont, for example, provides health care coverage for 10 years after an exonerated individual is released from prison.

In states without compensation laws, like Kansas, those who are exonerated typically have to file a lawsuit to get compensation or convince legislatures to pass a special appropriation to pay them. Lawsuits can be time-consuming, costly and challenging to win. And winning compensation from a legislature isn't guaranteed.

In Kansas, for example, a wrongfully convicted person currently must go to the Legislature's Special Claims Against the State Committee and plead for compensation.

Debate Over Amounts

How much people deserve for the time they lost behind bars often is in dispute. It was in Indiana this year.

Rep. Greg Steuerwald's bill would compensate individuals with $25,000 for every year of wrongful incarceration. Democratic Rep. Greg Porter thinks they should receive $35,000 for every year of imprisonment.

Both bills would award compensation only to people whose crimes were vacated through DNA analysis. The attorney general would be in charge of processing claims for wrongful conviction compensation, and neither bill would apply retroactively. But both bills appear dead for the year.

Frances Lee Watson, founder of the Wrongful Conviction Clinic at the Indiana University McKinney School of Law, said she hopes legislators will continue to push for compensation. "Convictions are still being vacated and people are still being exonerated in Indiana—but we don't have a compensation law," she said.

Another sticking point in trying to pass compensation laws is overcoming lawmakers' general faith in the criminal justice system or convincing them that innocent people can be convicted.

In nearby Michigan, Republican Gov. Rick Snyder signed a bill in December that pays $50,000 for each year of wrongful imprisonment and provides re-entry services after release. But the bill's sponsor, Democratic Sen. Steve Bieda, first introduced it in 2004.

"I think [legislators] had a hard time wrapping their heads around the fact that someone could spend so much time behind bars and not have done something wrong," Bieda said of his struggle to pass the bill. "I had to reintroduce [the legislation] again and again."

Lawmakers in other states are looking to tweak their compensation laws by streamlining payments or ensuring that some people aren't left out unfairly.

In Tennessee, for instance, Republican Rep. Mark Pody wants to make it easier for people who are innocent, but aren't exonerated by the state's parole board or the governor, to receive compensation. Why? A judge vacating a conviction is not enough for an individual to qualify for compensation under current law.

His bill would allow a wrongfully convicted individual to apply for compensation without an official exoneration after spending at least 25 years in prison and if the conviction was overturned by DNA evidence.

The bill wouldn't affect many people in Tennessee. But it would affect Lawrence McKinney, who was released from prison in July 2009 after 31 years based on new DNA evidence. McKinney was denied an official exoneration from the parole board and is currently awaiting a decision from Republican Gov. Bill Haslam.

Compensation in Kansas

After spending time on the Kansas Legislature's joint committee that decides on civil claims for wrongful conviction, Democratic Sen. David Haley decided he wanted to change how innocent people such as Floyd Bledsoe are compensated in his state to make it more just and evenhanded.

"Some [people] made compelling arguments," he said, "but there seemed to be no rhyme or reason as to who [was awarded] what."

So last month, he introduced a bill that would compensate wrongfully convicted individuals with $80,000 for each year spent in prison or $1 million if sentenced to death. It would also pay $5 million to the heir of an individual who was wrongfully executed, though the state hasn't conducted an execution since 1965.

The bill hasn't passed yet. There are questions about whether $80,000 is the right amount. And the bill has been amended to include some notable limitations: Individuals who pleaded guilty or no contest to a crime, for example, would not be eligible for compensation—even if the conviction was later vacated.

Sinha of the Innocence Project said provisions like this in compensation laws can deprive some innocent people of their rightful compensation because they were coerced, or saw little hope in winning at trial and agreed to a plea bargain.

The National Registry of Exonerations has confirmed over 350 instances of individuals who pleaded guilty to crimes they did not commit. According to the Innocence Project, nearly 11 percent of the nation's DNA exonerations involved innocent people pleading guilty.

Haley's bill in Kansas also would require people who are exonerated to apply for compensation within two years after their release from prison. That would exclude the bulk of people whose convictions have been vacated.

Bledsoe, whose brother committed the murder he spent time in prison for, doesn't want to be one of those people. But time is running out for him to get the level of compensation Haley thinks he deserves. Dec. 8 will mark two years since his release from prison.

"I haven't completely lost faith in our justice system," Bledsoe said. "[But] it's hard to trust in something that's not perfect."

15

The Changes in Media Coverage and Its Impact on Convictions

Liz Banks-Anderson

Liz Banks-Anderson is the media and communications coordinator for the University of Melbourne Law School in Australia.

The most recent wave of crime media coverage—including shows like Making a Murderer *and podcasts like* Serial—*has encouraged jurors and the general public to become more aware of the prevalence of wrongful convictions. It has also changed the societal discussion surrounding legal issues. Because of mainstream media coverage highlighting cases of miscarriages of justice, younger citizens are less likely to jump to conclusions when serving as jurors, which should result in fewer wrongful convictions in the future.*

A new wave of crime coverage is highlighting miscarriages of justice and changing the way we think about the judicial system.

Ten years ago the 'CSI effect' signified a shift amongst jurors to treat evidence with more scepticism. Now, a new disruptive force—the 'Serial' or 'Making a Murderer' effect—is changing the way the law is discussed in the mainstream.

University of Melbourne criminal law expert Professor Jeremy Gans says the cases highlighted in made-for-the-web documentary

"The 'Making a Murderer' Effect," by Liz Banks-Anderson, Pursuit, the University of Melbourne, March 16, 2016, https://pursuit.unimelb.edu.au/articles/editing-the-making -a-murderer-effect. Licensed under CC BY-ND 3.0 AU.

series, *Serial* and *Making a Murderer*, will break down barriers which impede access to information, as was the case with "old-style crime coverage, with a voice telling you what to think."

"I think there is going to be talk in a few years of a 'Serial' or 'Making a Murderer' effect—much like the 'CSI effect'—where you may see prosecutors complaining about jurors being a bit too sceptical," says Professor Gans, from the Melbourne Law School.

"People will get more used to the potential fallibility of the judicial system and be more willing to ask questions and look for things they were otherwise discouraged from looking for.

"Victoria has the world's best example of a case that went wrong because of DNA evidence—the Farah Jama case. Farah Jama was wrongly convicted of rape because of a contaminated DNA sample.

"I always argue that scepticism could have detected this wrongful conviction because the jurors in that case asked questions of the judge, which turned out to be the right questions to ask as they exposed this particular miscarriage of justice."

Professor Gans says the case of Steven Avery as shown in Netflix's *Making a Murderer* is fascinating.

"It seems much clearer to me that a terrible miscarriage of justice has occurred. Although you never really know why someone does commit a terrible crime like that (murder), it seems an incredibly implausible crime for Avery to get involved in at that point in his life," Professor Gans says.

He believes the monopoly that courts have on information is being lost due to the transformative effect of new media.

"Because these shows are surrounded by social media discussion, it will continue something which has already been happening, which is the breakdown of attempts to wall off jurors from the rest of the world—it is not going to be tenable.

"Whether this is a good or a bad thing is irrelevant because the process is not stoppable; it is the product of a current age. The average age of a judge is 60. The average age of jurors is 40. The next stage is the millennials who grew up with social media and you will never get past that."

This new wave of crime coverage began with *Serial,* a trial by podcast in which co-creators Sarah Koenig and Julie Snyder revisited the case of Adnan Syed, the US high school student convicted of the murder of his classmate and former girlfriend Hae Min Lee.

This was followed by Andrew Jarecki's *The Jinx*—a six-part HBO documentary that follows the case of New York real estate heir Robert Durst, acquitted in one murder case and awaiting trial in another.

Ten-episode Netflix docu-drama *Making a Murderer* examines the plight of Wisconsin man Steven Avery, who is serving a life sentence for a crime he says he did not commit.

In 1985 Avery was wrongly convicted for the sexual assault of a local woman. Avery was sentenced to 32 years in prison, serving 18 years before being exonerated by DNA testing, a technology introduced after his trial. This DNA also identified the attacker – a person of interest police declined to investigate. For this, Avery filed a lawsuit against Manitowoc County for $36 million.

In 2005 Avery was arrested again for the murder of 25-year-old photographer Teresa Halbach. His nephew Brendan Dassey was later arrested as well, after giving what his lawyers say was a coerced confession to helping Avery rape and murder her. In 2007, after separate trials, both were found guilty and sentenced to life in prison.

"There is no strong case against him and I am shocked the conviction succeeded and shocked that, absent of this documentary, it does not look like there would be a lot of moves to remedy this," Professor Gans says.

Shows like *Making a Murderer* are valuable because they put the spotlight on the legal system, he says.

"It breaks the idea that the justice system is adequate to its task and cannot get it terribly wrong. *Making a Murderer* shows us that every protection can fail simultaneously ... cases like Steven Avery's are continually highlighting how difficult it can be to apply the law to the human unknown.

There's a sobering moment in the series when an NBC producer discusses the Avery case and why it makes the perfect narrative: "It's a story with a twist, it grabs people's attention … Right now murder is hot, that's what everyone wants, and we're trying to beat out other networks to get that perfect murder story."

Crime investigations in the media are not new.

"It puts the spotlight on a particular miscarriage of justice, that would otherwise be lacking," Professor Gans says.

"Really, it is hard to break through people's willingness to accept quick summaries of cases. These detailed examinations can put a focus on a particular case. That's no small thing, because we are talking about a man who might have his life taken away."

Professor Gans says anywhere else in the world, including Australia, there would be calls for an enquiry into Steven Avery's case. Calls for a retrial, however, would require convincing a court to revisit the case.

"Obvious as it was (to me) from looking at the trials of Steven Avery and Brendan Dassey that there was not the case to convict them, they were convicted by a jury who based their decision on the same information I saw.

"It begs the question, why should millions of viewers who came to a conclusion override 12 people whose job it was to come to that conclusion at the time," he says.

"Really, the only way to convince the court to revisit the case would be to deliver an argument that outlines some sort of legal flaw in the trial or fresh evidence."

People critical of the documentary say the directors presented a biased perspective. Professor Gans says it is hard sometimes to know whether to trust the messages these documentaries put out as some can be too skewed in their analysis.

"Everything needs to be treated with caution because everyone has an agenda," he says. But what these documentaries, Professor Gans says, are showing us is that we need to be more cautious about trusting the process of the law when it is applied to the human unknown.

"There are so many aspects of this documentary I would not have believed had I not had the footage in front of me. There is a realisation that the world can be much weirder than you think. The difference between fiction and fact is that fiction has to be plausible," he says.

Organizations to Contact

The editors have compiled the following list of organizations concerned with the issues debated in this book. The descriptions are derived from materials provided by the organizations. All have publications or information available for interested readers. The list was compiled on the date of publication of the present volume; the information provided here may change. Be aware that many organizations take several weeks or longer to respond to inquiries, so allow as much time as possible.

The Center for American Progress
1333 H Street NW, 10th Floor
Washington, DC 20005
phone: (202) 682-1611
website: www.americanprogress.org

The Center for American Progress is an independent policy institute dedicated to improving the lives of all Americans. The institute maintains an informative website covering many issues, including those related to courts and criminal justice.

Centurion
1000 Herrontown Road
Princeton, NJ 08540
phone: (609) 921-6919
website: www.centurion.org

Centurion is a small but dedicated organization. Since 1983 they have worked to free wrongfully convicted people serving life or death sentences.

The Conversation
89 South Street, Suite 202
Boston, MA 02111
website: www.theconversation.com

The Conversation is an independent nonprofit network of newsrooms that identifies topics of concern and interest and then uses experts to comment on such issues. It addresses a wide variety of information about the topic of wrongful conviction.

CounterPunch
PO Box 228
Petrolia, CA 95558
phone: (707) 629-3683
email: counterpunch@counterpunch.org
website: www.counterpunch.org

CounterPunch is a left-leaning news website that aims to keep the public informed. They publish articles on a number of subjects, including social justice issues.

Grist
1201 Western Avenue, Suite 410
Seattle, WA 98101
phone: (206) 876-2020
website: www.grist.org

Grist is an independent news outlet. As an independent nonprofit news source, their journalists provide in-depth coverage of important topics including social justice issues.

The Innocence Project
40 Worth Street, Suite 701
New York, NY 10013
phone: (212) 364-5340
email: info@innocenceproject.org
website: www.innocenceproject.org

The Innocence Project was founded with two distinct goals in mind: to exonerate innocent individuals using DNA evidence and to reform the justice system in order to prevent future injustices.

The Nation
520 Eighth Avenue
New York, NY 10018
phone: (212) 209-5400
website: www.thenation.com

Founded by abolitionists in 1865, *The Nation* believes in debate about politics and culture with the aim of helping readers fight for justice for all. They believe in intellectual freedom, facts, and transparency.

The National Institute of Justice (NIJ)
810 Seventh Street, NW
Washington, DC 20531
phone: (202) 307-2942
website: www.nij.gov

The National Institute of Justice maintains a website with a vast amount of information on all aspects of wrongful convictions and exonerations.

The Pew Charitable Trusts
901 E Street NW
Washington, DC 20004-2008
phone: (202) 552-2000
email: media@pewtrusts.org
website: www.pewtrusts.org

The Pew Charitable Trusts is an independent nonprofit organization dedicated to serving the public. Pew publishes a magazine, *Trust*, four times a year that can be read online. Articles and information cover a vast array of topics, including the civil legal system.

Think Progress

PO Box 34716
Washington, DC 20043
phone: (202) 684–1030
email: general@thinkprogress.org
website: www.thinkprogress.org

ThinkProgress is a news site dedicated to rigorous reporting. They offer the latest information on pressing topics such as wrongful conviction.

Bibliography

Books

Laura Caldwell, *Anatomy of Innocence: Testimonies of the Wrongfully Convicted.* New York, NY: Liveright Publishing Corporation, 2017.

Michael D. Cicchini, *Convicting Avery: The Bizarre Laws and Broken System Behind Making a Murder.* Amherst, NY: Prometheus Books, 2017.

James M. Doyle, *True Witness: Cops, Courts, Science, and the Battle Against Misidentification.* New York, NY: Palgrave Macmillan, 2005.

Barry C. Feld, *Kids, Cops, and Confessions: Inside the Interrogation Room.* New York, NY: New York University Press, 2013.

Mark Godsey, *Blind Injustice: A Former Prosecutor Exposed the Psychology and Politics of Wrongful Convictions.* Oakland, CA: University of California Press, 2017.

Jon B. Gould, *The Innocence Commission: Preventing Wrongful Convictions and Restoring the Criminal Justice System.* New York, NY: New York University Press, 2008.

Anthony Graves, *Infinite Hope: How Wrongful Conviction, Solitary Confinement, and 12 Years on Death Row Failed to Kill My Soul.* Boston, MA: Beacon Press, 2018.

Robert Francis Kennedy, *Framed: Why Michael Skakel Spent Over a Decade in Prison for a Murder He Didn't Commit.* New York, NY: Skyhorse Publishing, 2016.

Corey Mitchell, *Murdered Innocents.* New York, NY: Pinnacle Books, 2016.

Erin E. Murphy, *Inside the Cell: The Dark Side of Forensic DNA.* New York, NY: Nation Books, 2015.

Elizabeth A. Murray, *Overturning Wrongful Convictions: Science Serving Justice.* Minneapolis, MN: 21ˢᵗ Century Books, 2015.

Peggy J. Parks, *DNA Evidence and Investigation.* San Diego, CA: Reference Point Press, 2010.

Stuart Taylor, *Until Proven Innocent: Political Correctness and the Shameful Injustices of the Duke Lacrosse Rape Case.* New York, NY: St. Martin's Press, 2007.

James L. Trainum, *How the Police Generate False Confessions: An Inside Looks at the Interrogation Room.* Lanham, MD: Rowman & Littlefield, 2016.

Tom Wells, *The Wrong Guys: Murder, False Confessions, and the Norfolk Four.* New York, NY: W. W. Norton, 2008.

Periodicals and Internet Sources

Laura Bazelon, "Justice After Injustice," Slate, September 30, 2015. https://slate.com/news-and-politics/2015/09/restorative-justice-for-false-convictions-crime-victims-and-exonerated-convicts-work-together.html.

Lauren Brooke Eisen and Inimai Chettiar, "39% of Prisoners Should Not Be in Prison," *TIME*, December 9, 2016. http://time.com/4596081/incarceration-report/.

Reuven Fenton, "Top Reasons People Are Imprisoned," *New York Post*, November 15, 2015. https://nypost.com/2015/11/15/top-reasons-people-are-falsely-imprisoned/.

Virginia Gordan, "Advocates for Exonerated Former Inmates Outraged Over Compensation Case Dismissals," NPR, February 22, 2018. http://www.michiganradio.org/post/advocates-exonerated-former-inmates-outraged-over-compensation-case-dismissals.

Jon Greenberg, "Watch Out, 70% of Us Have Done Something That Could Put Us in Jail," *PunditFact*, December 8, 2014.

https://www.politifact.com/punditfact/statements/2014
/dec/08/stephen-carter/watch-out-70-us-have-done
-something-could-put-us-j/.

John Grisham, "Commentary: Why the Innocent End Up in
Prison," *Chicago Tribune,* March 14, 2018. https://www
.chicagotribune.com/news/opinion/commentary/ct
-perspec-innocent-prisoners-innocence-project-death-row
-dna-testing-prosecutors-0315-story.html.

Samuel R. Gross, "The Staggering Number of Wrongful
Convictions in America," *Washington Post,* July 24, 2015.
https://www.washingtonpost.com/opinions/the-cost-of
-convicting-the-innocent/2015/07/24/260fc3a2-1aae-11e5
-93b7-5eddc056ad8a_story.html?utm_term=.f8175390d6e9.

Marti Hause and Ari Melber, "Jailed But Innocent: Record
Number of People Exonerated in 2015, *NBC News,*
November 21, 2014. https://www.nbcnews.com/news/us
-news/jailed-innocent-record-number-people-exonerated
-2015-n510196.

Celeste Headlee, "Life After Exoneration, For the Victims
on Both Sides," NPR, April 15, 2013. https://www.npr
.org/2013/04/15/177341744/life-after-exoneration-for-the
-victims-on-both-sides.

Jack Healy, "Wrongfully Convicted Often Find Their Record,
Unexpunged, Haunts Them," *New York Times,* May 5, 2013.
https://www.nytimes.com/2013/05/06/us/wrongfully
-convicted-find-their-record-haunts-them.html.

Virginia Hughes, "How Many People Are Wrongly Convicted.
Researchers Do the Math," *National Geographic,* April 28,
2014. https://www.nationalgeographic.com/science
/phenomena/2014/04/28/how-many-people-are-wrongly
-convicted-researchers-do-the-math/.

Kate King, "For Victims' Families, the Torment of Exoneration,"
Wall Street Journal, November 7, 2016. https://www

.wsj.com/articles/for-victims-families-the-torment-of
-exoneration-1478482579.

Stephanie Slifer, "How the Wrongfully Convicted Are
Compensated for Years Lost," *CBS News*, March 27, 2014.
https://www.cbsnews.com/news/how-the-wrongfully
-convicted-are-compensated/.

Peter Wagner and Wendy Sawyer, "Mass Incarceration: The
Whole Pie 2018," Prison Policy Initiative, March 14, 2018.
https://www.prisonpolicy.org/reports/pie2018.html.

Index